# 1942

## When British Rule in India Was Threatened

### Krishna Kumar

INDIA • SINGAPORE • MALAYSIA

ISBN  979-8-89133-829-6

The Rapid Reads book series is dedicated to my late parents, who taught me to be curious and self-analyze.

These and other forthcoming books are possible only because of the love and support of my family.

In 1942:

Speaking in Diet, the Japanese Parliament, General Tojo, the Japanese Prime Minister, said on February 15th:

*'Japan expects that India will regain its proper status as India for the Indians, and she would not stint herself in extending assistance to the patriotic efforts of the Indians'.*

Churchill wrote, in a letter to King George VI on February 24th:

*'Burma, Ceylon, Calcutta, and Madras in India and part of Australia may fall into enemy hands'.*

# ABOUT RAPID READS

Indian history is vast. Rapid reads about India is an attempt to present comprehensive details and analysis of a specific event or period in an authentic manner.

The developments are covered in a linear timeline, the way events happen in real life, so that a proper and honest assessment of the impact on our lives can be done.

# CONTENTS

# PEOPLE, COUNTRIES, CITY NAMES, ABBREVIATIONS, AND COLLOQUIAL USE

## People

1. Ambedkar, Dr. Bhim Rao: Leader of Depressed Classes. Member of Viceroy's council.

2. Amery, Leopold Charles: Secretary of State for India 1940-1945.

3. Atlee Clement Richard, Earl:British Prime Minister 1945-51, Member of Simon Commission, Deputy Prime Minister during WWII. Labor Party leader.

4. Auchinleck, Field Marshal Sir Claude:Commander in Chief, British Indian Army 1943-1947.

5. Ayer, S.A:Reuter's Correspondent to Southeast Asia, Propaganda, and Information Minister in Azad Hind Government, 1943-1945. Author of 'Unto Him a Witness.'

6. Azad, Maulana Abul Kalam:President Indian National Congress 1940-1946 Subsequently Minister of Education 1947-1958.

7. Bhonsle, J.K Major General: moved to I.N.A. from British Indian Army—Chief of Staff of Netaji.

8. Bose, Ras Behari: a Revolutionary who moved to Japan. Leader of India Independence Leagues in Southeast Asia.

9.  Bose, Sarat Chandra: Renowned Advocate, Freedom fighter, Member Constituent Assembly, Elder brother of Subhas Chandra Bose, and his key supporter.

10. Bose, Subhas Chandra: Leading Freedom Fighter, Congress President, First Prime Minister of Undivided India, and Commander in Chief of the Indian National Army.

11. Chennault, Claire: American flyer, Consultant to Chiang Kai Shek, leader of A.V.G. Group.

12. Churchill, Sir Winston Leonard Spencer: Noted India hawk. Leader of the Conservative party, Prime Minister of Britain 1940-1945.

13. Cripps, Sir Richard Stafford: a sole member of Mission to India in 1942 and member of cabinet Mission 1946.

14. Das, Chittaranjan: Mentor of Subhas Bose and revolutionary leader. Part of Congress Party. Had a huge following.

15. Desai, Bhulabhai: Renowned Bombay Lawyer, Congress leader but fell in Gandhiji's disfavor. Led the Red Fort trial defense and brought the I.N.A. story into the open.

16. Dhillon, G.S: Moved to I.N.A. from the British Indian Army—part of the trio for first I.N.A. Trials.

17. Huq Fazal-Ul: Leader of Praja Krishak Party and Chief Minister of Bengal.

18. Fujiwara, Iwaichi: A Japanese intelligence officer who helped form I.N.A. The coordinating group was, therefore, known as F. Kikan.

19. Gandhi, Mohandas Karamchand: Barrister, and Leader of the Indian National Congress, addressed as Mahatma or Gandhiji most

of the time in the book, as is usually done in India. (ji is a Hindi honorific).

20. George VI:British King and Emperor of India (among other dominions and occupied territories).

21. Hirohito, Showa: The Emperor of Japan.

22. Hitler, Adolf: Nazi Party leader and Chancellor of Germany.

23. Irvin, Lord: Also known as Lord Halifax, Viceroy of India. 1926-31 and British Foreign Secretary 1936-38.

24. Linlithgow, Lord Victor Alexander John:Viceroy of India 1936-1943.

25. Jinnah, Mohammed Ali:President of the Muslim League, First Governor General of Pakistan.

26. Kiani, M.Z Major General: Joined I.N.A. from the British Indian Army. Moved to Pakistan after Independence.

27. Khan, Shahnawaz, Colonel: Moved to I.N.A. from the British Indian Army. Trial in Red Court. Commission for inquiry into Netaji's death. Later Minister in Nehru's Cabinet.

28. Khan, Sikander Hayat: Chief Minister of Punjab and leader of the Unionist Party.

29. Mussolini, Benito: Italian Dictator 1922-1943.

30. Nehru, Jawahar Lal: Congress leader, Prime Minister of British India 1946-1947. First Prime Minister of India 1947-1964.

31. Patel, Sardar Vallabhbhai:Gandhian, Known as Iron Man for his firm will and uniting various princely estates and forging present-day India. Home minister in free India.

32. Percival, Arthur, Lt. General: British Commander in Malaya and Singapore.

33. Ribbentrop, Joachim Von: Nazi leader and Foreign Minister of Germany 1938-1945.

34. Roosevelt, Franklin Delano: President of the United States 1933-1945.

35. Sahgal, Prem Kumar: Moved to I.N.A. from the British Indian Army. Trial in Red Fort.

36. Saffrani, Abid Hasan: Travelled with Bose from Germany and became a diplomat in Independent India.

37. Savarkar, Vinayak Damodar:the Only person to be given two lifetime imprisonment, Social reformist and leader of Hindu Mahasabha, a Revolutionary and Freedom Fighter.

38. Singh, Mohan: Founder of I.N.A. after moving from the British Indian Army. After disagreements interned for the duration of the war, later Joined Congress, and became a Rajya Sabha member.

39. Schenkel, Emilie: Love interest and wife of Subhas Bose.

40. Slim, William, Lt General: later Field Marshal British Commander in Burma.

41. Shek, Chiang Kai: Premier Republic of China and later President of the Republic of China (Taiwan).

42. Tojo, Hideki:Japan's Minister of War and Prime Minister 1941-44.

43. Wavell, Field Marshal Sir Archibald Percival:Commander in Chief India 1941, Supreme Allied Commander South West Pacific December 1941-June 1943, Viceroy of India October 1943-1947.

44. Yamashita, Tomoyuki:Commander Japanese forces which occupied Malaya.

# Countries and names

1. Burma was Part of British India till 1937 and is now called Myanmar.

2. French Indo-China is Today's Cambodia, Vietnam and Laos

3. Malaya Earlier name for Malaysia

4. Siam is earlier name of Thailand

5. The Land of the Rising Sun is a popular name for Japan.

# Cities

1. Ahmednagar: City in Western India.

2. Allahabad: A city in North India, one of the earliest to come into direct British occupation, has a High court, University, and very active political life. Now, back to the original name,Prayagraj.

3. Bombay: Port City in Western India. One of the earliest British possessions has a high court and University and is the commercial capital of India. Very active political life in this period. She is now called Mumbai. The name was also used for State at that time.

4. Calcutta: British took an area Called Fort William on lease in the 1770s, and the city came up around, Capital of British India till 1911. She is now called Kolkata.

5. Dacca: City in Eastern India in Bengal, now the capital of Bangladesh.

6. Delhi/New Delhi: Twin Cities became the capital of British India in 1911—Present Capital of India.

7. Imphal:is the Largest City of Assam in Eastern India, near Burma.

8. Karachi: Port City, an important trading center in western India, is Now part of Pakistan.

9. Mandalay: An important city in Myanmar.

10. Madras:Now called Chennai. One of the earliest cities to come into British possession. It has a High court and university, and the name was also used for the State.

11. Poona: An Industrial city near Bombay, which is now called Pune.

12. Rangoon: the Capital city of Burma (Myanmar), Now called Yangon.

13. Shimla: A City in the Himalayas in North India. Now Spelled as Shimla. The summer capital of British India, where the government moved from Delhi.

14. Vizag Or Vishakhapatnam: a port town in Southeast India.

15. Wardha: Gandhiji's Ashram in Central India.

16. Sabarmati: Gandhiji's Ashram near Ahmedabad.

## Abbreviations/Colloquial use

1. AICC: All India Congress Committee.

2. B.B.C: British Broadcasting Corporation.

3. Congress: Indian National Congress, the main political party of British India.

4. League: Muslim League, A political party representing Muslims.

5. I.C.S.: Indian Civil Service that ran the administration of British India.

6. I.I.L.:India Independence League.

7. I.M.A.:Indian Military Academy at Dehradun.

8. I.N.A.:Indian National Army.

9. Mahasabha Hindu Mahasabha: a political party.

10. N.W.F.P.: Northwest Frontier Province, Now Known as K.P.K. and is in Pakistan.

11. P.O.W.: Prisoner of War.

12. R.A.F.: Royal Air Force.

13. R.I..N: Royal Indian Navy.

14. R.S.S.: Rashtriya Swayamsevak Sangh, A social organization.

15. The Raj: Colloquial name for British Rule.

## Notes

1. Various spelling, depending on citations from different authors and periods, are used for followers of Islam: Muslim, Mohammedan. So, it is used interchangeably.

2. A Few Citations are marginally minimally reworded to maintain context clarity and flow of language.

3. Highlights are mine.

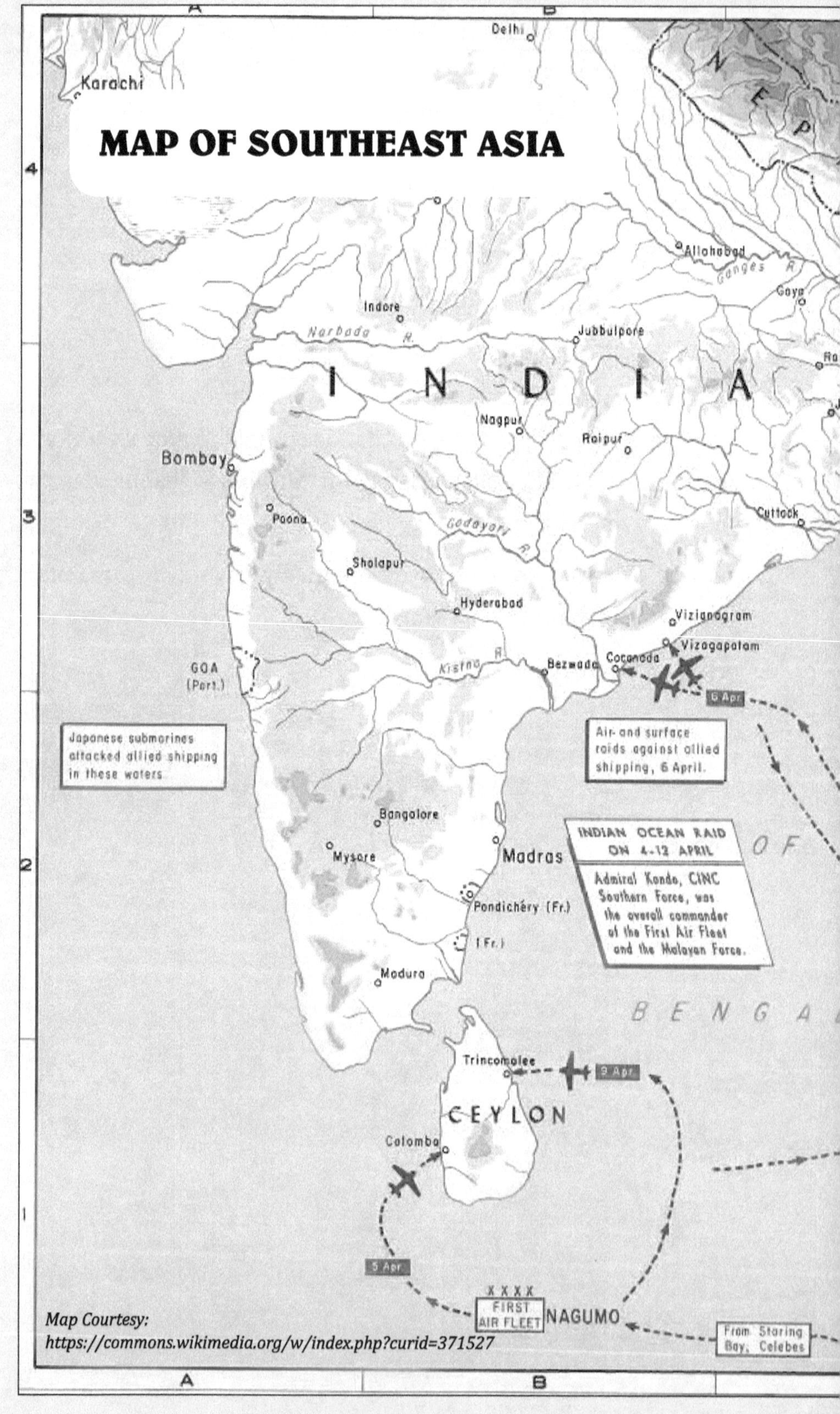

MAP OF SOUTHEAST ASIA
Karachi
Delhi
NEP
Allahabad
Ganges R.
Goya
Indore
Narbada R.
Jubbulpore
Ra
I N D I A
Nagpur
Raipur
Bombay
Cuttack
Poona
Godavary R.
Sholapur
Hyderabad
Vizianagram
Vizagapatam
Kistna R.
Bezwada
Cocanada
6 Apr
GOA
(Port.)
Air- and surface
raids against allied
shipping, 6 April.
Japanese submarines
attacked allied shipping
in these waters.
Bangalore
INDIAN OCEAN RAID
ON 4-12 APRIL
Mysore
Madras
Admiral Kondo, CINC
Southern Force, was
the overall commander
of the First Air Fleet
and the Malayan Force.
Pondichéry (Fr.)
OF
(Fr.)
Madura
B E N G A
Trincomalee
9 Apr
CEYLON
Colombo
FIRST
AIR FLEET
X X X X
NAGUMO
From Staring
Bay, Celebes
5 Apr

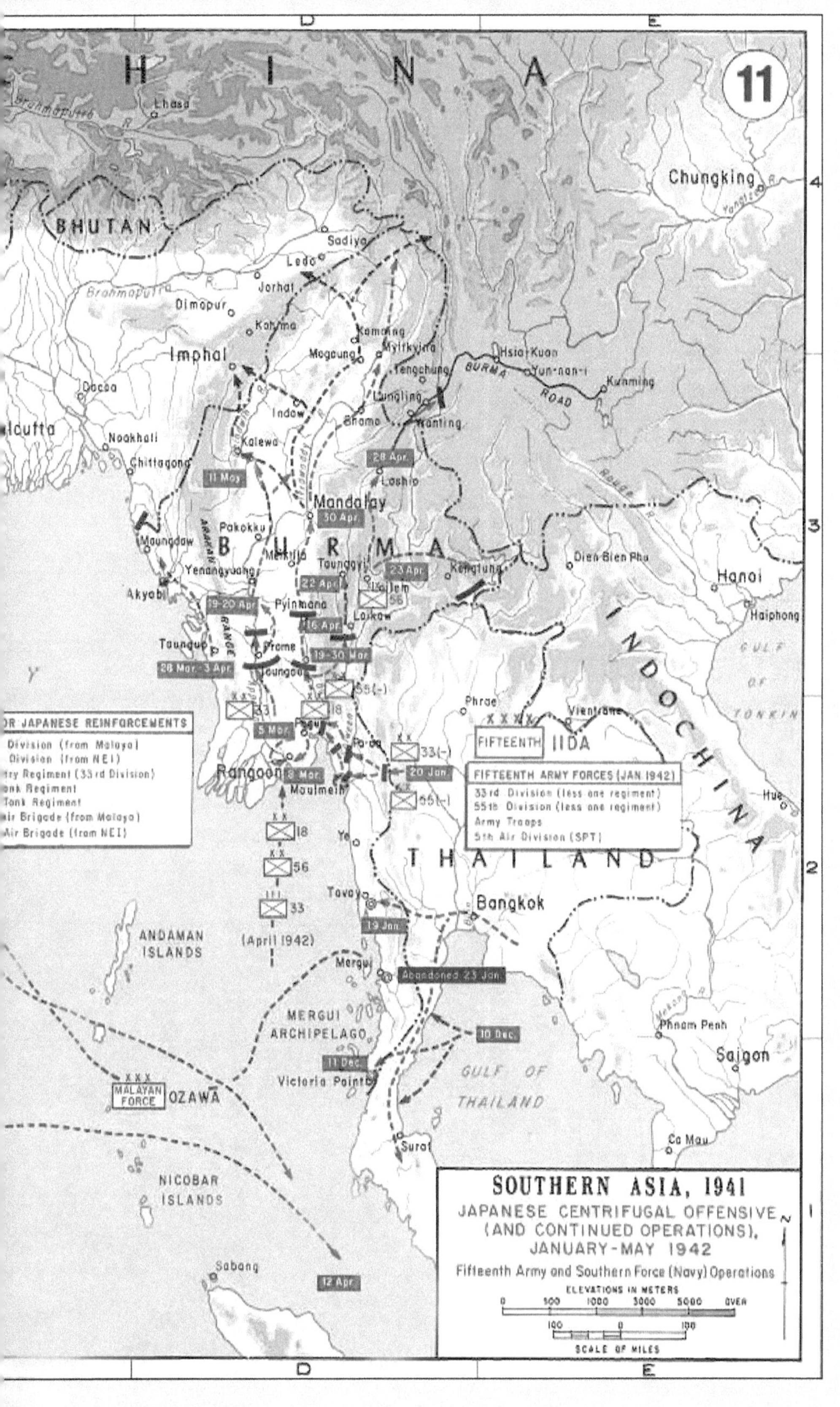

CHINA
BHUTAN
Lhasa
Brahmaputra R.
Chungking
Yangtze R.
Sadiya
Ledo
Jorhat
Dimapur
Kohima
Imphal
Dacca
Kamaing
Mogaung
Myitkyina
Tengchung
Hsiar Kuan
Yun-nan-i
Kunming
BURMA ROAD
Lungling
Bhamo
Wanting
Salween R.
Calcutta
Noakhali
Indaw
Chittagong
Kalewa
28 Apr.
Lashio
11 Mar.
Maungdaw
Pakokku
Mandalay
30 Apr.
23 Apr.
Kengtung
Dien Bien Phu
Hanoi
BURMA
Yenangyaung
Meiktila
Taunggyi
Loilem
56
Haiphong
Akyab
19-20 Apr.
Pyinmana
22 Apr.
Loikaw
GULF
OF
TONKIN
ARAKAN YOMA RANGE
16 Apr.
Prome
19-30 Mar.
55(−)
Phrae
INDOCHINA
Taungup
Toungoo
28 Mar.-3 Apr.
33
18
Pegu
55(−)
Vientiane
FIFTEENTH
IIDA
5 Mar.
Rangoon
8 Mar.
Moulmein
Paan
33(−)
20 Jan.
FIFTEENTH ARMY FORCES (JAN.1942)
55(−)
33rd Division (less one regiment)
55th Division (less one regiment)
Army Troops
5th Air Division (SPT)
Hue
18
Ye
56
THAILAND
33
Tavoy
Bangkok
(April 1942)
19 Jan.
ANDAMAN
ISLANDS
Mergui
Abandoned 23 Jan.
10 Dec.
Phnom Penh
MERGUI
ARCHIPELAGO
Saigon
11 Dec.
Victoria Point
GULF OF THAILAND
Mekong R.
Ca Mau
XXX
MALAYAN
FORCE
OZAWA
NICOBAR
ISLANDS
Surat
Sabang
12 Apr.


OR JAPANESE REINFORCEMENTS
Division (from Malaya)
Division (from NEI)
try Regiment (33rd Division)
ank Regiment
Tank Regiment
ir Brigade (from Malaya)
Air Brigade (from NEI)


SOUTHERN ASIA, 1941
JAPANESE CENTRIFUGAL OFFENSIVE
(AND CONTINUED OPERATIONS),
JANUARY-MAY 1942
Fifteenth Army and Southern Force (Navy) Operations
ELEVATIONS IN METERS
0    500   1000   3000   5000   OVER
100        0        100
SCALE OF MILES


11

# CHAPTER 1

# INTRODUCTION

By the time Marquess Wellesley was recalled by the East India Company in 1805, he had put a considerable part of India under the direct rule of the British as well as subsidiary alliances with most of the native rulers, allowing for British dominance in India. It kept increasing steadily, and when the British Crown took over the East India Company, the claim of the Empress of India held good for Queen Victoria of England.

India was squeezed to the maximum extent possible. An estimate for this period is that between one-fourth to one-third of the annual revenue of the Government of India was sent to England as home charges, besides sky-high salaries for British serving in India, high rates of returns from money invested in projects like Railways, and so on.

In 1921, the New York Times said,' *British Imperialism would be compelled to evacuate Great Britain itself before it would willingly evacuate India.*'[1] India was tightly controlled with oppressive laws imposed via a bureaucracy whose will was forced by the police and army.

India supplied soldiers, support staff, and people for all parts of the British Empire.

During World War II, by 1942, soldiers under arms for the British were around a million[1], with more being recruited daily. Indian factories were in overdrive, producing goods for the Empire at the cost of depriving the population.

British rule in India faced 1942 as its most turbulent and challenging year since 1857 when what the British call the sepoy rebellion and what Indians consider the first War of Independence had taken place.

Let us review the British defense doctrine to understand this. The priorities given to the army were not as these exist today.

In 1933, the Garran Tribunal was set up to examine the role of the Army and its funding. The Garran Award of 1933 defined the primary role of the army as follows:

'The duties of the army in India include the preservation of internal security in India, the covering of the lines of internal communication, and the protection of India against external attack. Though the scale of the forces is not calculated to meet an external attack by a Great Power, their duties might well comprise the *initial resistance of such an attack pending the arrival of Imperial reinforcements.*'[2]

To put it in simple language, if India was to be attacked by the Soviet Union, which was the major British concern at this time- Indian forces were to hold the invader till assistance came from England as size, technology, and means with the Indian army were not sufficient.

Under Chatfield committee, the role of the Army defined in 1939 was:

'a. To maintain law and order in India and to suppress any possible rebellion.

---

[1] By the end of the war this figure had reached around 2.5 million.

b.  To maintain the status quo vis-a-vis the tribes on the North West Frontier.

c.  In Cooperation with the air force and the navy, to beat off sporadic attacks by hostile naval or air force.

d.  To defend India against the attacks of a minor power like Afghanistan, and

e.  To defend the Imperial outposts in the Middle East and *Far East Area as bastions of India's external defense'.*[3]

This highlights the priorities and goals of the army very clearly. *The army was a tool of oppression while in India and a tool to defend the British rule elsewhere.*

Throughout history, any Empire has survived only as long as it could project its power. The power could be real or imagined, but it must be believable by its subjects.

The year 1942 was when the British lost a large part of this power projection. Another event followed this- the formation of I.N.A.- that formed the basis of the eventual dismantling of the British Empire on which the sun never set.

The British war prowess in India had given them the image of being invincible. Their training methods, the discipline of the troops, and assured regular monthly payment of the salaries coupled with wins against princes and global deputations (which started in 1790) had created a mystique and aura of the British Indian Army. This aura and the army were powerful tools in controlling the population in British India, and the significant reasons, besides the police force and administration, were that a small number of Britishers could control a vast and spread-out population. The army was used to maintain control over the princely states and assist the administration in suppressing dissent.

The first dent in this aura of invincibility came when Britain itself came under threat by Luftwaffe bombing, the threat of invasion and naval blockades by U-2 Boats, and struggling for survival, lost Singapore, Malaya, Hongkong, and Burma in Asia.

The debacle of Singapore and Malaya in 1942 was a decisive loss to the British and demonstrated a poor strategy and inadequate fighting ability,

The areas from Hong Kong to Burma were very tightly linked with India when under the British.

The British officers were interchanged in these places with India.

Trade in Hong Kong, Singapore, Malaya, and Burma was substantially in the hands of Indian traders.

The defense of these areas was under the responsibility of the Government of India as per the Chatfield Doctrine. The British army at these places had predominantly Indian soldiers but British and Australian officers.

Malaya and Singapore had large numbers of labor and supervisory positions with Indians.

Therefore, what happened in these areas became known to people in India very quickly and also caused an impact in India.

The second dent was the return of troops from Burma and the information coming from there about the treatment of British officers of their Indian troops, along with the inability to face the Japanese. The British had constantly underrated the Japanese and their fighting ability without paying close attention and placing enough value on Samurai Ethos and the Bushido code of the warrior.

When the Japanese took over Burma, tired, dejected, and defeated, almost 100,000 British army soldiers came to India. Some were evacuated by air, some by motor vehicles or ships others, mostly Indians, walked through the dense jungles of Assam. Further, almost 400,000 civilians crossed over to India, many dying due to harsh terrain and indifferent evacuation arrangements.

Burma, till 1937, was part of India and managed from Calcutta. Even in 1942, Rangoon and Mandalay had regular ferry service from Calcutta and a large number of Indians in trade and labor.

Another factor was that the British pooled resources. Each place had resources unique to that place, which were collectively exploited. If Hong Kong was the traditional trading point with China, then Singapore was the point where about 25% of the Empire's trade passed and was a major naval center. Malaya produced most of the tin and rubber for the Empire, and Burma was a significant source of Oil and Rice.[2].

As there were Indian traders and also workmen everywhere, events of one place necessarily impacted another. Linked to all of them was India, where the people living in these places still maintained active links and often loyalty as well.

The third dent was when the Japanese bombed the Indian cities of Calcutta, Madras, Vizag, and Kakinada. Many Ships were sunk while in the harbor. Evacuation started from Coastal Cities, and ports on the Eastern side were closed for shipping.

After the Bombing of Madras, the British started to make plans to even evacuate from India, worried that the Japanese attack might come into full force. Because of focus on Northwest area for defense of India,

---

[2.] Burma was the second-largest exporter of Rice in the world at that time.

the British were simply not organized for meeting an onslaught from Northeast.

At the same time, to continue with British rule, the British strategy was to offer Indians increased involvement in administration, and Sir Stafford Cripps was sent to India.

The failure of this mission, loss of membership of Congress, and being ignored by the British after the provincial government resignations gave rise to the Congress party launching a do-or-die agitation, later named as 'Quit India.'

This became the fourth dent when the Congress party launched its agitation and protest in August '42.

Thus, as never before, India's British rule came under external and internal threats.

The common person in India was amazed at these happenings and found one surprise after another during this year.

The Japanese threat of naval blockade or further bombing of India was over when Japan suffered setbacks in the Pacific.

The monsoon stopped the possibility of a land invasion of India from Burma.

The August '42 agitation of Congress was suppressed with brutal repression within two months of launch.

Thus, things were beginning to change in favor of the British by the end of the year. However, Malaya, Singapore, Hongkong, and Burma did not return to British control till '45.

The fifth dent, which eventually became the fatal blow to the Empire, was Subhas Chandra Bose, who had escaped from India and formed the Indian National Army in Germany, followed by the formation of the Indian National Army in Southeast Asia in '42. Later, when Subhas Chandra Bose took over this army, he energized the soldiers and increased their inspiration and commitment to nationalism, which became legendary.

The Indian National Army became the slow fuse that exploded the gunpowder of dissent and suppression in and ignited the whole of India in '45-'46 and forced Britain to leave India. Soon, one by one, countries forming the Empire had to be vacated, and in the next twenty years, the Empire was over.

The seed of British rule's collapse in India and the British empire was sown with the events of 1942, and this book traces that.

# CHAPTER 2

# BRITISH DEBACLE IN SOUTHEAST ASIA

On October 4[th,] 1940, Japan joined the Axis powers Germany and Italy, who were already at war with the Allies, i.e., Britain, France, and other European powers.

While Germany was trying to increase its boundaries under the concept of lebensraum[3]- the living space -Imperial Japan, which also had territorial and raw material sourcing ambitions, was already fighting a war with China and now defined its extended area of interest throughout the region.

In 1940, Japan formally declared the Greater East Asia Co-Prosperity Sphere or GCEAOP. Besides Japan, it included Korea, Manchukuo, the Pacific Islands, Southeast Asia, and Burma. Burma had just been separated from British India in 1937. It had become an independent country technically, though still under the British.

This declaration put the Japanese directly in conflict with the British- whose Empire in Asia extended from Hong Kong to India. Thailand was independent. Australia and New Zealand were British dominions. Indochina was under the Vichy Government of France.

---

[3.] Under this concept, Nazi Germany claimed various territories to seek living space for Germans.

The countries of the British Empire were closely linked with trade connections among themselves. Further, Indian and Chinese merchants ran the business from Burma to Singapore. Indian labor was employed in Malaya and Singapore, and the mid-level supervisory staff was often Indian as well. Almost three-quarters of a million Indians lived in Malaya. Singapore had areas where the significant population was Indian. Serangoon Road in Singapore continues to be a mini-India to date.

The British so far had only been indirectly involved in China's war as they were supplying along with the United States Generalissimo Chiang Kai Shek, whose Army had retreated to Chun King. This route is what became famous as *Burma Road.* It involved supplies first reaching Rangoon via sea and then moving overland to Lashio and Chunking. With the blockade of Hong Kong, this route was of great importance.

India had extensive trade with Japan. It was a significant source of raw cotton for Japan. Japanese textiles, bicycles, electric goods, etc., were imported into India.

At the end of 1941, India had almost 900,000 men under arms. Over 300,000 had been sent overseas to the Middle East, Iraq, and Malaya. The balance in India included some 150,000 on watch and ward on the Northeast Frontier and on internal security duty throughout the country. Approximately 300,000 were undergoing recruit training at training centers; the remainder were in field formations and administrative units being raised. Recruits were being taken in at the average rate of 50,000 per month.[4]

The British did not feel that Japan was likely to attack Singapore or Hong Kong, and only marginal armed forces were allotted to these places. In the British Indian Army, the experienced soldiers were deputed to the west. Therefore, the soldiers in Southeast Asia, besides being inadequately equipped under British officers, were primarily new recruits; some of the officers could not speak Hindi/Urdu, and soldiers did not have battle condition experience. Hongkong was guarded by six battalions, two each were of British, Canadian, and Indian origin. There was inadequate airpower and limited artillery.

Malaya was a flourishing economy. 'In 1940, the Governor of Singapore estimated that Malaya was 'worth' an estimated £227.5[4] million to the British Empire. Its exports were £131.5 million, of which £93 million went to foreign countries, especially to the United States, to which it sold more than any other territory of the British Empire.[5] Besides, Malaya had a huge opium factory. Say historians Bayly and Harper, 'the British Crescent was supported by narco colonialism on a colossal scale'.[6]

Penang, the largest city of Malaya, had Indian, Chinese, and Malay inhabitants besides those of mixed races as well. Technically, Malay rulers were sovereigns, but a combination of flattery, strong arm, gifts, etc., ensured that the British held sway.

Malaya's command was under Lieutenant General Arthur Percival, who had ten infantry brigades under him. The troops were ill-organized, under-equipped, and ill-trained.

Singapore was the cornerstone of the British Empire due to its location, and almost twenty-five percent of the Empire's trade passed through the peninsula. It was a substantial naval base as well. Singapore was a quintessential Raj town with British, Chinese, Indians, and Malays, including Arabs and Japanese, populating its half-a-million population and the well-known Raffles hotel catering mainly to the British and

---

4. Present value: $23165 Million approx.

expatriates. It was a truly cosmopolitan city with Hindus, Muslims, Christians, Parsees, and their places of worship.

Churchill, in 1939, had asserted that Singapore was a stepping stone to Australia and New Zealand. Sir John Dill, chief of the Imperial General Staff, said this was the most important strategic point in the British Empire.[7]

'Hankey asserted what became the conventional wisdom, the loss of Singapore would be a calamity of the first magnitude. We might well lose India, and the faith in us of Australia and New Zealand would be shattered. If Britain ceded mastery in the East to Japan, General Smuts warned the Dominions office in 1934,' she would go the way the Roman Empire had gone.'

But by 1939, it seemed that the immense naval station constructed on the northeastern side of the island, facing the Johore Strait, which provided twenty -two square miles of deep-sea anchorage, could counteract the local superiority of the Japanese fleet.[8]

Singapore was well fortified from a sea attack, as an attack from Malaya was considered impractical. The port had batteries, adequate ammunition, guns capable of delivering a lethal blow to opponents, etc.

Singapore's garrison consisted of soldiers from many parts of the Empire. 'Sturdy British infantrymen, Scottish Highlanders, Bronzed young giants from Australia, tall, bearded Sikhs, Muslim rifleman fresh from service on the Northwest frontier, tough little Gurkhas, Malays from the Malay regiment. The uniforms in the streets, the persistent drone of airplanes overhead, the wail of sirens to signal air raid drills, the nocturnal spectacle of searchlights playing over the water, the overwhelming presence of the Royal Navy -all proclaimed that Singapore was the 'the core of the British strength in the far East.'[9] This however, soon proved to be an illusion.

British Army commander in Malaya Lieutenant General Lionel Bond had conceded in 1940 that the defense of Singapore demanded the defense of the entire Malay peninsula…The British soldiers tended to think of the peninsula as an impenetrable jungle; it was not…Bond also realized that a naval presence alone would be insufficient to deter a Japanese invasion, nor were the fabled big guns effective in land warfare. They could be rotated inwards, but they only had armor-piercing shells for use against ships; the heaviest 15-inch guns had no high explosive rounds for use against artillery or infantry.[10]

Bond had estimated that he needed between thirty-nine and forty-two infantry battalions. With sufficient air support, that might be reduced to twenty-five. Still, some 336 first-line aircraft were required… in September 1940, there were only ninety first-line Aircraft in Malaya, mostly aging Brewster Buffaloes, the flying beer that had been rejected for service in Europe. In Indochina, the Japanese had concentrated 600 combat-ready planes. Churchill insisted that the visible presence of the Royal Navy would be enough to deter any aggressor. A further symbolic gesture was therefore made. In late October 1941, a small flotilla Force Z was assembled under Vice Admiral Tom Phillips. It included the navy's most modern battleship, the *Prince of Wales*… with one of the oldest battlecruisers, *Repulse*, and four destroyers. There were no aircraft carriers.

On December 7th, 1941, Japan entered World War II simultaneously in the Pacific by attacking Pearl Harbor, one of the Hawaii Islands, and thus attacking the United States and Asia by attacking Malaya, The Philippines, and Hong Kong, all within seven hours.

The Pearl Harbor attack came a few minutes before 8 a.m. on Sunday, the 7th. Four battleships were blown up or sank, four battleships were damaged, and eleven others were sunk or disabled. Airfields were attacked, and 188 aircraft were destroyed on the ground.

On the same day, Japanese Aircraft destroyed seven British Aircraft in Hong Kong. Only one survived.

The Japanese attack on Malaya was spearheaded by General Tomoyuki Yamashita, a daring General. Like many Japanese officers, he was an ardent student of the German military system. In 1940 as head of a military mission, he had gone to Germany to observe the methods employed in Hitler's lightning conquest at close range,[5] of the continent. In 1941 and 1942, he adapted some of these practices to inflict the most stunning defeat the British Empire suffered in the entire war. Miracles were not strange to him; he accomplished one in the jungles of Malaya.[11]

Yamashita had announced that he would be in Singapore by New Year's Day. He was well briefed on British weaknesses.[12]

The Japanese began landings at 1: 35 AM on December 8th at Kota Bahru. In one day, sixty Allied planes were put out of action.[13].

'Shenton Thomas's initial reaction to the landings would later haunt his memory. I suppose you will shove the little man off. He is said to have commented. The British had been blinded by racial assumptions that the Japanese were small, myopic, and with a level of military achievements below that even of the Italians. But the allied commanders were soon to concede that the Japanese were far tougher than their own troops.'[14]

Japanese troops from the 25th Army landed in Malaya from the northern border of Thailand and swiftly brought destruction

---

[5.] Germany had run over France and Western Europe with a strategy called Blitzkrieg which involved fast-moving mechanized units occupying the country end to end, ending military opposition while bypassing cities that were occupied later.

throughout the region. and began the occupation using the strategy of 'bicycle blitzkrieg' when thousands of soldiers moved into proximity of Singapore on bicycles.

The British Indian forces were simply no match, with inadequate armaments and a lack of training. Besides, the Japanese were able to bomb the area freely. 'The Japanese troops were battle-hardened (with experience in the China war which had been going on for some time), and the Indian troops defending Malaya were raw and without experience. Further, the British movements were by motor vehicles and hence restricted to main roads. At the same time, the Japanese on bicycles traveled through the side roads and plantations.

'On December 10th eighty-four Japanese torpedo-carrying aircraft spotted by chance and then sank the British battleship *Prince of Wales* and her sister ship *Repulse.* In all, 840 officers and men drowned, and 1285 survivors were picked up from the sea. The two warships, Malaya's only serious naval defense, had been on their way as decided by their commander at the last moment to attack a Japanese Naval force that had begun to put troops ashore at Kuantan.'[15]

'After three days of war, the Japanese were effective masters of both the South China Sea and the Pacific Ocean. In their attack on the two British War ships, only four of the eighty-four Japanese Aircraft had been shot down.'[16]

'The sea lanes to Ceylon, India, and Darwin lay open and unprotected.'[17]

'The moral collapse of British rule in Southeast Asia came not at Singapore but at Penang. The retreat through Perak had left Britain's oldest possession in Malaya extended. It was a fortress with a devoted 'fortress commander.' But the decision was taken not to defend it.

This gave the Japanese assault when it came on December 9th and 10th a terrible surreal quality. For the first two days, Japanese planes flew reconnaissance missions unchallenged…However, on Thursday, December 11th, the planes attacked with bombs and almost continuous machine gun fire.'[18]

'Describes an English Doctor Oscar Fisher' The general hospital was overwhelmed by around 700 casualties of these; 126 died in the first twenty-four hours. No anesthetist was available, and amputations were carried out in the conditions of a nineteenth-century battlefield… the stench of gangrene was appalling… bodies lay on the streets after the city's capitulation. The resident commissioner estimated the number of dead and injured at 3000; some 1000 lay under the rubble. Army disposal units were overcome by the stench, even wearing gas masks. Then came cholera and typhoid.'[19]

The Japanese kept moving inside, and soon an event occurred which has much significance in Indian History, Major Iwaichi Fujiwara of the intelligence department of the Imperial Japanese Army, with the assistance of Sardar Pritam Singh, leader of India Independence League of Bangkok. met a Prisoner of War, Major Mohan Singh, and they soon formed F. Kikan, which later became Indian National Army. More on this in a later chapter.

On December 18th, the Japanese landed on Hong Kong Island. Soon one by one, all islands were occupied and by. 'On December 25th, Hong Kong surrendered, thus becoming the first British Possession to fall under the emblem of the Rising Sun. 11000 British soldiers were taken prisoners.'[20] The Indian divisions had been practically annihilated and had borne the brunt of the attack.

On the evening of December 24th, General Mac Arthur, who was in the Philippines, left Manila for the island of Corregidor.[21]

'For the battle of Malaya was all but over. Australian and Indian troops along the Johore line fighting hard and at great cost of lives slowed the Japanese advance but did not stop it…. Yamashita's Imperial guards broke resistance in the west after barely a week. What had been billed as the 'main battle' for Malaya was lost.' [22]

'Wavell returned to Singapore and afterward, on January 14th, broke the news to Churchill that there was no 'fortress at Singapore; the fixed defenses of the island were virtually non-existent. Churchill was horrified. He told the chiefs of staff this was one of the greatest possible scandals that could possibly be exposed.'[23]

Churchill refused the surrender initially; ultimately, it was permitted.

Singapore surrendered on February 15th, 1942. General Percival, who was the commanding officer, surrendered. 'At this time, the British forces outnumbered the Japanese three to one. Japanese General Yamashita had only thirty thousand men and was almost out of ammunition and food. His supply lines were badly clogged and stretched back hundreds of miles. Japanese troops, already living on two bowls of rice a day, faced starvation unless the fortress surrendered promptly.'[24]

Describes historian Brendon 'As it happened Percival so bungled his dispositions that he handed victory to the Japanese on a plate. Having dispersed his troops around the shore, he placed the weakest formations in the northwest where the Johore Strait narrowed to a thousand yards, and the landings duly took place. He kept central reserve to counterattack.'[25]

When the British surrendered, 130,000 were taken prisoners. Some of the Indians among these were later to join Indian National Army. Besides Indians, the Singapore surrender to the Japanese included the British, Australians, and others.

The European Civilians in Singapore had an especially tough time. Throughout the Empire, they were used to the chit system where they signed small pieces of paper for the purchases and services and did not carry cash, and now suddenly, cash was needed as the chit system stopped operating.

The Japanese invasion of Singapore Island was a gigantic and wholly successful piece of bluff.[26]

Describes Shahnawaz Khan, who was in the British Indian Army and later in I.N.A. His commanding officer Major McAdam, had final words with him on the morning of February 16th 'I suppose this is parting of our ways.'

'The next day, some 40,000 Indian troops were concentrated at Farrer Park, a small stadium near the Indian center of Singapore, Serangoon Road. There is considerable debate about what occurred here and its significance. There was a perfunctory speech from a British officer Colonel Hunt who told the assembled that they were prisoners of war and had been turned over to the Japanese. Some Indian officers recollected that he had said: Now you belong to the Japanese Army. 'This was to be a critical point for those who claimed that the Indian National Army, which fought alongside the Japanese, was a legitimate force. Rumors of Hunt's alleged speech were also heard in India and spread the conviction that the Raj was tumbling towards its end. Hunt then left. Fujiwara spoke, in Japanese, which was translated into English, then Hindustani. He told the troops that they would not be treated as *prisoners but as brothers...*[27].

The shock of Singapore's fall was felt well beyond the Orient. It even reverberated in the remote recesses of the Northwest Frontier (in India), where Pathans expressed' disdain that so grave a reverse should have been suffered at the hands of such foes.'[28]

The fall of Singapore, 'the Gibraltar of the East,' was a serious blow to Britain's ability to resist Japan and also a severe blow to British morale. 'Here is the moment,' Churchill told the British people in a broadcast on February 15th, to display the calm and poise, combined with grim determination, which not long ago brought us out of the very jaws of death. The only real danger Churchill warned would be a weakening in our purpose and, therefore, in our unity -that is the mortal crime'. Whatever was guilty of such a crime or of bringing it to others, 'it was better for him that a milestone was hanged about his neck and he was cast into the sea.'[29]

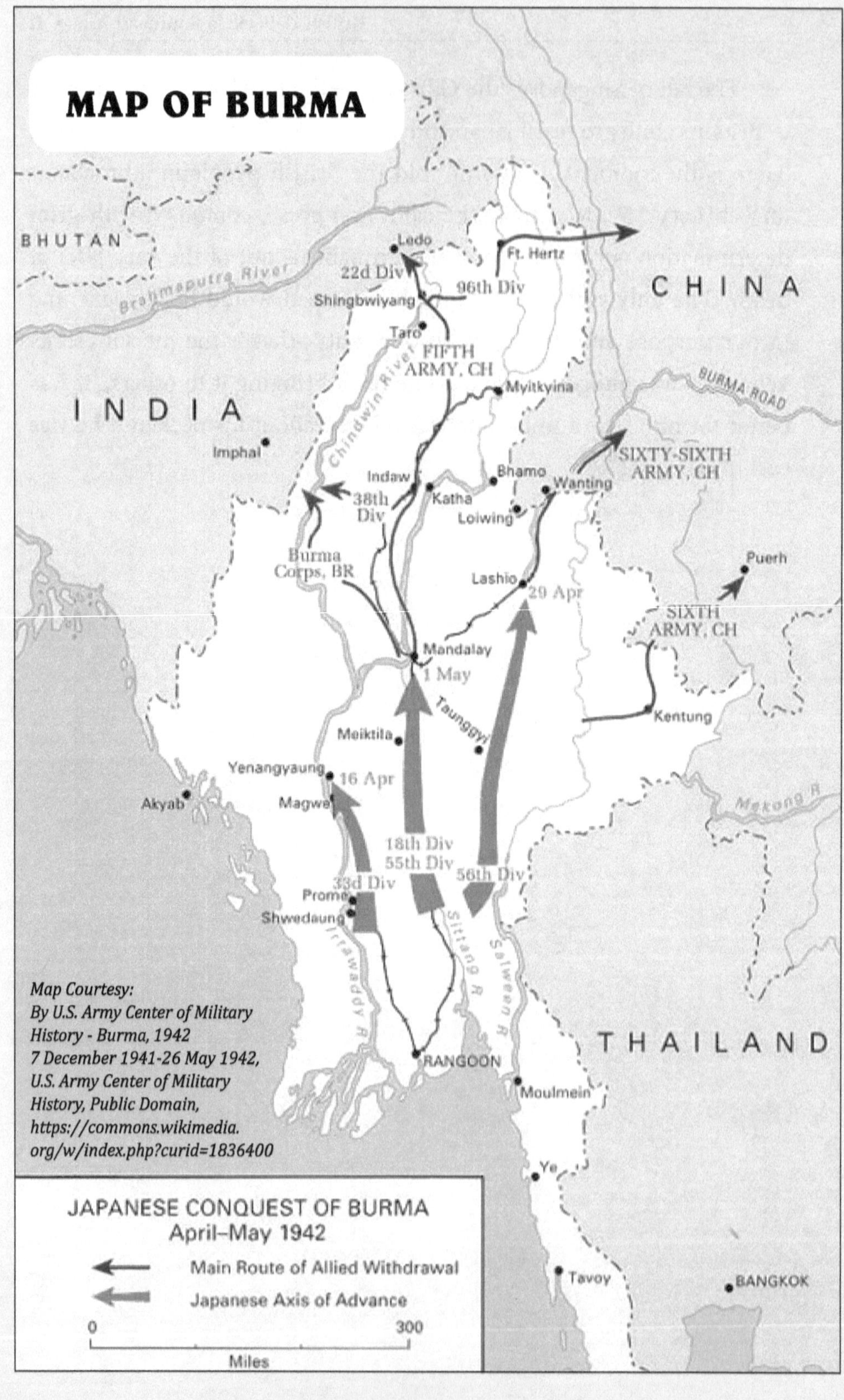

MAP OF BURMA
BHUTAN
Brahmaputra River
CHINA
INDIA
Ledo
22d Div
96th Div
Shingbwiyang
Ft. Hertz
Taro
FIFTH
ARMY, CH
Myitkyina
BURMA ROAD
Imphal
Chindwin River
Indaw
Katha
Bhamo
Wanting
SIXTY-SIXTH
ARMY, CH
38th
Div
Loiwing
Burma
Corps, BR
Lashio
Puerh
29 Apr
SIXTH
ARMY, CH
Mandalay
1 May
Taunggyi
Kentung
Meiktila
Yenangyaung
16 Apr
Magwe
Akyab
18th Div
55th Div
56th Div
Mekong R.
33d Div
Prome
Shwedaung
Irrawaddy R.
Sittang R.
Salween R.
RANGOON
THAILAND
Moulmein
Map Courtesy:
By U.S. Army Center of Military
History - Burma, 1942
7 December 1941-26 May 1942,
U.S. Army Center of Military
History, Public Domain,
https://commons.wikimedia.
org/w/index.php?curid=1836400
Ye
JAPANESE CONQUEST OF BURMA
April–May 1942
Main Route of Allied Withdrawal
Japanese Axis of Advance
Tavoy
BANGKOK
0
300
Miles

# CHAPTER 3

# BRITISH LOSE BURMA

An invasion of India's northeast frontier across the grain of the country had never been visualized because of the distance of any possible enemy, the difficulties of the terrain, and the fact that such communications, as there were in Burma, ran north and south. The traditional threat had always been from the Indian northwest, and India's defenses had been planned to meet it.[30].

Burma had borders with India -Bengal and Manipur, Siam (Thailand), China, and French Indochina (which consisted of modern-day Laos, Cambodia, and Vietnam). Burma has an extensive mountain range and dense jungles. Three major rivers, the Irrawaddy[6], The Salween, and The Sittang, flow through it. Chindwin is a tributary of Irrawaddy, which is 1200 miles long and empties in the Bay of Bengal. Besides, there are many other smaller rivers.

The Japanese objective to occupy Burma, which was part of the Greater Asia Co-prosperity sphere, was simple. It was economic and strategic. At that time, Burma was the world's largest rice exporter, with a 37% share of global rice production. It is estimated that 63 percent of Burma's rice production was exported. It was also a significant

---

6. The name is derived from Sanskrit and means land of refreshment.

oil producer. Burma also offered teak wood, and the Burma teak is considered among the most durable and strong wood and was especially valuable in shipbuilding.

Besides, cutting off the Burma Road would deprive China, which was fighting a war with Japan, of U.S. and British supplies. When the Japanese occupied Canton[7] in 1938, the Hong Kong supply route was blocked, and now there were only three other options, which were Via Lachow or Via Yunnan in French Indo-China, and the Burma Road, which took products to Kunming and Chunking in China.

Rangoon was the largest city and a major port, with a population of around half a million. It was linked by shipping service to Calcutta and Madras. The second big city was Mandalay, and then the tribes were mainly distributed in hilly areas.

Several tribal people are identified as Burman. These are Kachin's, Karen's, and Shan's. Besides, there was a large population of Indians, Chinese, Anglo- Indians, and Anglo-Burmans.

Burma's primary monsoon season is from mid-May to mid-October, with extremely heavy rains in coastal and mountain areas. Malaria is common in many parts.

Indochina was a French territory. France was under Hitler and run by the Vichy Government, and hence, the Japanese Army was given access and facilities. Japanese also physically occupied Saigon and some other areas.

The Japanese had planned well. 'To preside over the conquest of Southeast Asia, a headquarters for the Japanese Southern Army was established at Saigon under the command of Count Teruauchi. The southern army comprised four smaller armies: XIV Army was to invade

---

[7] Shanghai

the Philippines. XV was to take Thailand to Burma. XXV army was to seize Malaya. XVI army was to overrun the Dutch East Indies.[31]

XV army had seen action in China, and 'in the early hours of December 8th, assault landings were made on the coast of Thailand and North-East Malaya. In conjunction with the landings from the sea, the Imperial Guards division entered Thailand from Indochina. The 55th Division's 143rd regiment was part of the Malayan invasion fleet but steered away northwards from the main convoys to make an opposed landing on the coast of Thailand between Chumphon and Pracuab.

By the morning of December 8th, the Thai premier and the Japanese Ambassador had reached an agreement to permit Japanese forces to pass across Thai territory.[32]

Later in December, the Thai and Japanese Governments signed a Treaty of Mutual Assistance[33]. Thus, Thailand came under Japanese influence.

Burma was part of British Far East command but by 1941's end, placed in General Head Quarters India command of Field Marshall Wavell after his strong representation to place it in India. Indian command was under him at that time, and he later became the Viceroy of India. 'As Burma had never been regarded as liable to attack by a major power, only minimal regular forces had been maintained in the country after her separation from India. These consisted of two British battalions, four battalions of the Burma Rifles, a small engineering works service on loan from India, a mountain battery, and a field company. These units were primarily located in the Rangoon and Maymyo districts. The force on which Burma chiefly relied, both for her internal security and for watch and ward on her land frontiers, was the Burma Military Police consisting of nine battalions. After the separation from India, six of these had been converted into the Burma Frontier Force (B.F.F.), but they remained under civil control. The Burma Auxiliary Force (B.A.F.) was also composed of volunteers recruited from the European, Anglo-Burmese, and Anglo-Indian communities.[34]

There were two regular British battalions, though with depleted strengths. There was inadequate air force. In the '40-'41 period, several more Brigades were sought to be formed, and two brigades were sent from India. Most of the troops, as elsewhere, were ill-trained and needed to become more familiar with the terrain. These were recently raised and sent to the battlefield due to the urgency and demand of the situation.

Japan started air raids on Burma in December end. The British had few fighter squadrons and could destroy only some Japanese Bombers while suffering losses.

The immediate consequence of the air raids was that Indian dock laborers and others decided to leave for India by using all routes, mainly overland. 'The air ministry program for the defense of Burma reckoned on six fighters, Seven bombers, and two army cooperation squadrons, a total of sixteen squadrons. In fact, only one A.V.G. Squadron, three fighter squadrons, three bomber squadrons, two army cooperation squadrons, and part of a general reconnaissance squadron joined the action.[35]. Meanwhile, troops kept coming from India, some of whom were only partially trained.

A.V.G. was the American Volunteer Group. This was led by Claire Chennault, an American who was an advisor to Chiang Kai Shek and had formed this group with 100 Fighters of P-40B Tomahawk. They defended Burma Road and also used the Burmese airfields.

The Japanese land invasion of Burma began in right earnest on January 20th, 1942. Almost immediately, the British started losing territory and evacuating. The first to fall to the Japanese at the end of January was Moulmein, one of the five largest cities.

One by one, the British regiments suffered devastating losses, and by the end of February, Rangoon had fallen. The Japanese had used airpower to catastrophic effect. After an attack on Magwe, the Royal Airforce was almost entirely destroyed by the end of March.

General Hutton, the British commander in Burma, was replaced by General Alexander.

Concerned about the closure of the Burma Road, Chiang Kai Shek, who had been fighting with the Japanese in China, offered Chinese troops, which the British did not accept initially but later accepted under pressure from the United States, and these were deployed under the command of Lt. General Stilwell.

Then in March '42, the command was passed on to experienced Lt. General William Slim. He tried to take on the Japanese, but by mid-March, he was completely surrounded by Japanese troops and had to request a retreat. The British started moving to India, destroying the oil fields.

Meanwhile, General Alexander realized that northern Burma could not be held. He ordered a withdrawal as well.

Complicating the situation was a large number of Indian civilians who lived in Burma.

Many of these decided to return to India, and some were evacuated by sea but mainly by road, which was highly treacherous terrain. There were hardly any amenities en route, and there is an estimate that around 50,000 Indians perished in the escape effort. Rangoon had people leave since January, and by the end of February, all but essential skeleton staff and certain administrative sections of Army headquarters had left.[36]

On March 6[th,] General Hutton decided that holding Rangoon was impossible. Destruction was started to demolish the oil refinery and storage tanks, power stations, and important buildings. Due to a shortage of engineering troops, many of the equipment and workshops remained undamaged. Large timber stocks, Coal, Steel rails, and building materials remained behind.

The last train left Rangoon on March 7th, and three ships left for Calcutta. The last naval ship left on March 8th.[37] At about mid-day on March 8[th,] the Japanese entered the unoccupied and deserted Rangoon.

Says Warren: 'The unrecorded death toll of the civilian population, whether from disease or acts of violence, would certainly exceed that of the combatant armies.'[38]

Meanwhile, R.A.F. was already moving airmen to India as well. The Japanese had used airpower to devastating effect. By the end of March, the Royal Airforce, after an attack on Magwe, was almost completely destroyed. 'The Japanese air force had achieved complete control of the skies of Southern and Central Burma.'[39]

The returnees faced roadblocks and were also harassed by low-flying Japanese aircraft that bombed and machine-gunned the returning soldiers.

On April 5th, 1942, the Japanese bombed Colombo and sank two British Cruisers, *Dorsetshire* and *Cornwall*, the armed merchant Cruiser *Hector* and the destroyer *Tenedos*. More than five hundred men were drowned. A Further three hundred men died when the aircraft carrier Hermes and the destroyer *Vampire* were bombed and sunk at Trincomalee[8]. During the same raid, twenty-three merchant ships were sunk in the Bay of Bengal, with a total of 112,000 tons lost.[40]

---

8. A port in Ceylon

On April 13th Japanese bombers struck the Burmese city of Mandalay. Two thousand people were killed, and much of the city was set on fire.[41]

On April 29th Japanese forces seized Lashio, the terminus of the Burma Road through which American and British supplies were being sent to China. On April 27[th,] as the Japanese grip on Burma intensified, General Stilwell sought permission, now that his position inside China was untenable, to withdraw to India, taking with him the 100,000 Chinese troops under his command. Washington authorized his withdrawal on April 30th. Four days later, the British were forced to abandon the port of Akyab on the Bay of Bengal, less than a hundred miles from the borders of India.[42]

'When a soldier of the 2nd Royal Tanks was asked how warfare in Burma compared with North Africa, he replied, 'Much the same amount of shit flying around, but the trouble with these Japanese bastards is that they don't run away like the Italians.'[43]

When the allied positions collapsed in Burma, the question was where to go: China or India? But the way the war developed, a retreat became impossible to go to China, and they ended up in India.

'The war's destruction, to be sure, exposed cracks in the imperial armor. Having raised the Rising Sun over Singapore, Japan Marched on to take Burma and made it to the threshold of India. There its sweep ended though not because of British strength alone. A monsoon deluged supply lines: without that and other accidental factors, India might have fallen to the Japanese, and the region's history would have gone in a very different direction.'[44]

Says historian Wilson 'the Raj's greatest failure was the rapid collapse of British rule in Burma. India's Eastern neighbor had been under the British government since the late nineteenth century, governed separately from the rest of the subcontinent only since

1937. The imperial regime in Burma was based on isolated European outposts, weakly connected by Burmese Collaborators and a dense network of Indian merchants. This structure collapsed quickly when faced with Japan's military machine. *In the monsoon of 1942, British and Indian troops trudged back with perhaps 140,000 civilian refugees. Army drivers were so weak from starvation many could not maneuver heavy Chevrolet trucks, and dozens fell into ravines.* The British government's relief policy was heavily biased in favor of the Europeans. As in Malaya, once Europeans were evacuated, British officers thought there was no one left to defend. All vehicles in Malaya, Singapore, and Burma were commandeered by white Britons. Wounded soldiers were left without treatment. *Between 50,000 and 100,000 people died of disease while trekking slowly through the mosquito-infested tracts on India's Eastern frontier.*[45]

Describes historian Elkins' Indians of all religions, races, and castes saw defeated white troops making their way back from Singapore, Malaya, and Burma to Calcutta Via Assam. Disease-ridden and demoralized members of the Indian Army *shared stories of the heroic and disciplined Japanese who defeated imperialist Britain in battle after battle.*[46]

Describe Bayly and Harper: 'The Indians, Anglo-Indians, and a small number of British trapped at Shingbwiyang sat out the drenching monsoon of 1942 in the camp without medicines, hope or for long periods food. Many died of malaria, malnutrition, blackwater fever, or maggot-infested sores before the survivors were rescued by jeep or elephant in October as the rains cleared. *These tales of despair and betrayal were never erased even by the striking British victories of 1944.*'[47]

'Over 400,000 refugees made the trek by land from Burma to India. One hundred and ninety thousand people reached Imphal via Tamu after crossing the Chindwin River. Thousands more trekked through northern Burma to Ledo and Assam. These poor wretches suffered the full force of the monsoon in the Hukawang Valley.[48]

Later in 1942, a military campaign to regain Burma by land from Northeast India seemed a formidable undertaking. Churchill would reflect that. 'Going into swampy jungles to fight the Japanese is like going into the water to fight a shark.'[49]

This was the second dent in the British aura of invincibility.

# CHAPTER 4

# INDIA BOMBED

The third dent in the aura of British invincibility was caused by the Japanese bombing of India in 1942 and the British reaction to it. *The panic that started in the British administration and people was one of cowardice in the eyes of Indians when the British began making plans to evacuate from India.* The ports of Eastern India were shut, and British men sent their families to interior areas. Further, it brought out in the open the inadequacy of the Royal Navy, which had always been projected as globally all-powerful and a significant factor in the creation of the global British Empire.

An India that had sent hundreds of thousands of army men to global war but had just eight anti-aircraft guns for its own defense was virtually indefensible at this time. The trained army had been sent to the western and African front, and the British Indian army remaining in India was raw and required practice. There were inadequate aircraft, and naval forces were insufficient as well. All that the army was capable of – was oppressing the unarmed, defenseless civilians.

India had not faced any external aggression in almost two hundred years. The Last major aggression was of Ahmad Shah Abdali in the 1760s. Even the defense of India doctrine was based on defense in

Northwest India as the British had conflicts with Afghans in the past and felt danger from the Soviet Union. There were no plans to defend against the Eastern border, and even the requisite supply network did not exist in this part. The borders of India on the eastern side touched Siam till 1937 before the separation of Burma. The British India borders were with Tibbat,Burma and Nepal, none of whom were hostile.

With Burma in possession of the Japanese along with Malaya and in agreement with Siam (Thailand), the Japanese effectively controlled the sea lanes and northeast land route to India besides air supremacy.

After surrendering in Singapore, the Royal Navy created a base in Ceylon. This was a strategic location at the southern tip of the subcontinent. Colombo was a huge seaport, and its location was such that it handled substantial cargo. To date, feeder vessels from multiple ports in India take or bring cargo to Colombo for onward shipment to the US or Europe or vice versa, and the big ships save on docking at multiple ports and changing routes.

'The admiralty had done its best to build up the Eastern Fleet despite heavy commitments and losses in the war against the European Axis. By late March, Sommerville's fleet at Ceylon comprised the modernized battleship *Warspite*, Four elderly Royal Sovereign class battleships, the new fleet aircraft carriers *Indomitable* and *Formidable*, the old aircraft Carrier *Hermes*, two heavy cruisers, five light cruisers, sixteen destroyers, and seven submarines.'[50]

After losing battleships *Prince of Wales* and *Repulse,* the British had suffered further losses when they lost heavy cruiser *Exeter, Aircraft* carrier *Ark Royal,* and battleship *Barham.* Additionally, battleships *Queen Elizabeth* and *Valiant* had been damaged.

Yamamoto had started working on plans for India and Ceylon right after the victory in Malaya. 'On March 9th, Yamamoto appointed Vice Admiral Kondo to command the operation against Ceylon. Kondo was to have two subordinate task forces, Vice Admiral Nagumo's aircraft carrier task force and Vice-Admiral Ozawa's detachment of cruisers and destroyers.'[51]

'Nagumo's carriers, *Akagi, Zaukaku, Shokaku, Soryu* and Hiryu, were supported by four battleships, two heavy cruisers, one light cruiser, and eleven destroyers. Half a dozen submarines were already on a reconnaissance patrol in the Bay of Bengal. An air strike on Ceylon was timed for April 5th.'[52]

Meanwhile, the attack in the Indian subcontinent started with the Andaman Islands. On March 23rd, the Andaman Islands were occupied by the Japanese. The British had evacuated these earlier after the fall of Rangoon as these islands were about five hundred miles from Burma, while from mainland India it is more than twice the distance.

These islands were to become the first Indian territory of the Azad Hind Government of Netaji Subhas Chandra Bose when the Japanese transferred these to him in November 1943. Ross Island in this group is now named after Netaji Subhas Chandra Bose.

'Ozawa's five heavy cruisers, one light cruiser, and eleven destroyers were accompanied by the light aircraft carrier *Ryujo*. They waited south of Andaman Island for action to commence.'[53]

'One hundred and twenty-seven fighter and bomber aircraft took off from Nagumo's carrier on April 5th, Easter Sunday, and reached Colombo. On a day when visibility was poor due to thunderclouds, showers, and mist, the dive bombers started the bombing. Destroyer

*Tenedos* and armed merchant cruiser *Hector* were first to go, followed by Submarine depot ship *Lucia.*'[54]

'By afternoon *Cornwall* and *Dorsetshire* were sunk.'[55]

'Next day, Nagumo's forces attacked the second port of Ceylon-Trincomalee. This lethal raid took care of *Hermes,* the aircraft carrier and destroyer *Vampire.*'[56]

'Admiral Nagumo now decided to stop the operations in the Indian Ocean.'[57]

'Meanwhile, Admiral Ozawa's task force swept across the Bay of Bengal towards the eastern coast of India. On April 6th *Ryujo's* aircraft bombed Vizagapatam and Coconada. Panic and alarm spread along India's eastern Seaboard. An air raid warning at Madras caused a general exodus. The 19th Indian division was concentrated on defending the coastline near the city. Major-General G.N. Molesworth recalled that there were so few anti-aircraft guns in India that near Madras and Vizagapatam, palm trees were cut down and the trunks stuck up at an angle of forty-five degrees in the hope that Japanese planes would mistake them for defenses. Churchill and the Chiefs of Staff in London had been anxious that the Japanese might invade Ceylon, but they did not think there was much risk to the Madras region as long as Ceylon remained in British possession.'[58]

'At sea Ozawa's force sank twenty-three merchant ships totaling 112,000 tons from April 4th to April 9th. There were further shipping losses at this time to Japanese submarines operating on the West Coast of India. The port of Calcutta became crowded with merchantmen unable to sail.'[59]

The remaining British eastern fleet was sent to Bombay, and Ceylon was abandoned. The Japanese had returned as there had to be increased effort in the Pacific due to increase in activities from the United States.

'From October 1942, the Japanese carried out occasional raids on airfields in Assam, Manipur and South-Eastern Bengal. The first night raid took place on Calcutta at the end of December.'[60]

Arrangements were made to destroy anything militarily useful in the city of Calcutta. Boats throughout Bengal which might have assisted Japanese invaders, were burnt, destroying the usual means by which the food was supplied throughout the province. British government officers sent their families to the hills. Indian officers moved them in with families elsewhere in India.[61]

'The fear spread that Japan was planning to land after Japanese warships sank a couple of merchant vessels. But the Japanese ships had gone back, and since the British did not know this, they closed all merchant shipping. As a result, all ports of eastern India – Calcutta, Vizag, and Madras were closed, leaving only Bombay and Karachi to handle all the traffic now.[62] The ports on the Eastern side of India were to reopen later.'[63]

Following the Japanese air raids of April 6th, 1942, on Vizagapatam 'the railways were practically paralyzed, and all the subordinate staff and labor fled from the place.. all provision shops were closed, and practically everyone deserted the town. The Port labor fled, and so did the coolies employed in constructing the new aerodrome.[64]

'In Vizag, hundreds of yards of trenches had been built over the preceding months to shelter people from air raids. For the convenience of the Japanese, the trenches had been built in neat, straight lines. The bombers just flew straight up them, dropping their load and creating havoc on the terrified population. Several ships were sunk in the harbor.[65]

In Madras, the prospect of invasion seemed to be so imminent that Government officers were moved to towns scattered throughout the interior, and the big cats in the City's Zoo were killed to stop them from rampaging after the inevitable attack.[66]

Describes *Wolpert 'British officials of Madras had all been swiftly evacuated to safety, but no thought was given to evacuating civilians or arranging for their transport, housing, and food supplies. It is the misfortune of India at this crisis in her history not only to have a foreign government but a government which was incompetent and incapable of organizing her defense properly or of providing for the safety and essential needs of her people.'*[67]

At their meeting at the end of April 1942, the All India Congress Committee charged that the 'officials whose duty was to protect the lives and interests of the people in their respective areal…ran away from their post of duty and sought safety for themselves, having the vast majority of people wholly unprovided for…. Such arrangements for evacuation, as were made, were meant for the European population.[68]

*By the middle of 1942, the Government was drawing plans to retreat from India and lead the fighting against Japan from Australia.* Indians withdrew their savings from British-run banks and could not even trust paper money, so started to collect small coins.[69]

'As a Women's Army Corps (India) officer later wrote of the military chaos of 1942, 'if the Japanese had known, one division landed in the south of India in late 1942 would have been unstoppable.'[70]

Churchill was to claim later that the British defended India from Japan! The fact remains that the defense of India was inadequate and making Government of India responsible for defense from Hong Kong to Egypt was much too much.

On February 24th, Churchill wrote, in a letter to King George VI, 'Burma, Ceylon, Calcutta, and Madras in India and part of Australia may fall into enemy hands.'[71]

In his dispatch, General Wavell called it 'India's most dangerous hour.'[72]

# Chapter 5

# SEEDS FOR COLLAPSE

The planting of seeds for the collapse of British Rule in India, which was done in 1942, survived and germinated. The attempts to plant and nurture the seeds had occurred since the 18th Century. The first enormous effort was in 1857 and then in 1906 when the Gadar party tried to make an effort from the U.S. and on a smaller scale in the First World War rebellion of soldiers. The Gadar party efforts failed because it was infiltrated by traitors with loyalty to MI 5 the British secret service. Besides, the individual efforts of revolutionaries had been in plenty, and some of the Congress party agitations/protests are covered in the next chapter.

During the First World War, Indian Army soldiers had been promised help by Germans. The Kaiser[9] had even written to Indian princes individually, offering support against the British.

Says Gilbert in his book on World War I: 'On February 15th, Indian soldiers in barracks at Singapore mutinied. and thirty-nine Europeans were killed. It was the first large-scale mutiny of the war. It was intended by its organizers as part of a general uprising by Sikh Militants against the British in India. The uprising had been encouraged by the Germans,

---

[9.] Official designation of the Imperial German Rulers.

who hoped that India was ripe for revolution, just as two weeks earlier, they had expected the Egyptians to be ready to overthrow the British once the Turks crossed the Suez Canal. A German ship, *the Bayern*, which had earlier been interned by the Italians, was found to be carrying half a million revolvers, 100,000 rifles, and 200,000 cases of ammunition, possibly for the uprising in India. The Sikh militants had certainly expected German help of this sort.'[73].

'In Singapore, British soldiers were called upon to carry out the executions of the ringleaders. Thirty-seven of them were shot. In India, the uprising was betrayed by a police spy, and the ringleaders were arrested before they could give the signal for revolt. Eighteen of them were hanged.'[74]

The inference was clear. Soldiers of the British Indian army were open to revolting against the British. It failed in World War I but showed it could be done on a bigger scale with the right motivation, inspiring leadership, and clear strategy. Subhas Bose provided that.

Thus, the efforts of 1942 become notable because even though these were initially started outside India, they were preserved against heavy odds. Soon, in '45-'46, when the Indian National Army was brought back to India, and soldiers were put to trial, it led to such a wave of protests/strikes and agitations that the country became ungovernable by the British, and they had to leave India.

The loss of India made the Global British rule impossible to continue. In about twenty years after Indian Independence, the Empire was over.

Two notable incidents stand out from 1942, which led to this seeding of freedom struggle.

The first is the actions of Subhas Chandra Bose in Germany, inspiring Indians and forming the Indian National Army.

Second is the formation and evolution of Mohan Singh, Pritam Singh, and Fujiwara's group from F.Kikan to the Indian National Army.

Subhas Bose was a charismatic presence in the Indian political scene. Having been jailed 11 times by the British between 1921-1931, he was exiled to Europe in February '33 and again arrested on his return in '36. One British intelligence report of 1929 described Bose as the *'most dangerous of the extremists' leaders in Bengal.'*[75]

Refusing to join after qualifying for I.C.S., choosing a life of seeking independence for Mother India, and being prepared to live a life of deprivation and suffering had given him a vast aura. His family was largely Anglicized, but he was a devoted worshipper of Ma Kali[10] and always remained connected to his roots.

Those who worked with him frequently praised him. The statement of S.A. Ayer, earlier the chief correspondent of Reuters during World War II in Southeast Asia and later a minister in Azad Hind Government, is indicative: *'I worship Netaji. To me, he is India's savior...'*[76]

He attracted such a devoted following that it was almost a cult where the worship was to Mother India, and the chief priest was Bose. His followers, even today, feel the same way. He is remembered, admired in the media and discourse, and recently his statue was inaugurated on Kartavya Path.[11] – the boulevard that links various locations and centers of the Indian Government. His statue was placed in a canopy that earlier had a statue of George V, and the place had been lying vacant since 1965 when British King George V's statue was defaced by some people.

Perhaps Ayer's description is very apt to mention here: *'The human relationship between Netaji and his soldier was thus unique. Each was*

---

10. Hindu Goddess who is the destroyer of Evil.
11. Road of obligations or commitment.

*prepared to do anything for the other. It was truly a hypnotized army, and it hypnotized him, too.*[77].

Even Sarojini Naidu, a Gandhian and on the opposite side of ideology with Bose, had this to say in 1945 *'His proud, importunate, and violent spirit was a flaming sword forever unsheathed in defense of the land he worshipped with such surpassing devotion'.*[78]

Bose had been elected president of the Congress party twice. First in 1938, when Gandhi was looking for a steady hand on the tiller, and second in 1939, when Gandhiji opposed him and put up his nominee against Bose. Bose, in 1938, had proved his mettle by organizing and asking the Congress Chief Ministers to work on planning to resurrect the Indian economy.

*'Congress ministers in the different provinces should, while they are in office, introduce schemes of reconstruction in the spheres of education, health, prohibition, prison reforms, irrigation, industry, land reform, workers welfare, etc.'*[79]

His vision of warfare in 1940 was clear:

*'Today, Britain can hardly call herself 'the Mistress of the Seas.' Her phenomenal rise in the 18th and 19th centuries was the result of her sea power. Her decline as an Empire in the 20th Century will be the outcome of the emergence of a new factor in world history -the Airforce.'*[80]

He had proved his administrative ability during the short period when he was mayor of Calcutta and chief executive of Calcutta corporation in the 1920s by settling industrial disputes and making organizational changes.

Bose had public differences with Gandhiji on various issues, including the response to freedom fighters, their approach to dealing with the British, and appeasement policies. He had been even prohibited from holding any office in Congress party for three years in 1940 after he formed Forward Block. Gandhi and Nehru often opposed him, but that did not diminish his popularity with the common person.

Bose had proved his ability to work without any religious preferences. He was thus able to work with both sides of the religious aisle. Indian National Army had Hindus, Muslims, Christians, Anglo -Indians, Sikhs, and Parsees, with virtually all religions of India represented therein.

His philosophy for seeking independence is what put him in direct conflict with Gandhiji. However, he remained in Congress, which at this time had people who were fighting for freedom though they followed different ideologies.

*Bose's strategy, determined in 1921, which he would follow for the rest of his life, was to use **all means to fight for freedom.***

Components of his strategy, therefore, were as stated by him:

*'If the members of the services withdraw their allegiance or even show a desire to do so, then and then only will the bureaucratic machine collapse.'*[81]

*'I have come to believe, further, that the national liberty which we want cannot be attained without paying for it dearly in the way of sacrifice and suffering. Therefore, those of us who have the heart to feel and the opportunity to suffer should come forward with their offering.'*[82]

He was clear about taking aid from Germany or other foreign forces for the freedom of India.

*'When the Army of Liberation was to attack the British Army in India 'When we do so, the revolution will break out not only among the civil population at home but also among the Indian Army, which is now standing under the British flag. When the British Government is thus attacked from both sides, from inside and from outside, it will collapse...'*[83]

In the ideological spectrum, Bose was just one step separate from the revolutionaries. He Had realized that *'British officers were always frightened by revolutionary violence.'*[84]

He should be ideally called prudent revolutionary as he generated fear with his actions and intellect in the British rule and he kept his focus on removing the rule completely much like teaching of Chanakya

He had actively supported revolutionaries in Bengal. Had led the funeral procession of Jatin Das, bare feet when he was Mayor of Calcutta, had supported the cause of Bhagat Singh. Praising Bhagat Singh, Bose said, *'Therefore I appeal to the brave Sikhs to produce more patriots having the courage and spirit of sacrifice of Bhagat Singh.'*[85]

In 1940 he was jailed for protesting against Holwell Monument[12] In Calcutta. World War II was ongoing, and the British were in no mood to release him. Bose decided that he had to get out -first did a hunger strike to be released from jail. He had decided to go to Germany and Italy and move plans for Indian Independence forward.

"Somebody had to be the emissary, somebody well-known who would be taken seriously. *'At last,'* he says, *'I decided to get out of India.*[86]

*Bose now thought of himself as India's man of destiny.*[87]

Why would Bose go abroad and fight for freedom? He was a man who was fond of studying history. In the First World War, Indian troops attempted a rebellion against the British. Besides, he was in constant touch with other revolutionaries. He had discussions with Veer Savarkar, who was a revolutionary, and it is widely believed that Bose was inspired by his idea to carry on the fight from abroad. It is also possible that this confirmed his concept as Subhas had been a student of military history

---

12. Holwell was East India Company's Calcutta head in the 1750s, whose narration about the black hole incident was used to attack Siraj.

and would indeed have known about the incidents during the First World War. In the earlier periods also when East India Company had armies based on the Presidency system there had been multiple smaller rebellions. 1857 was not the first, it was the largest rebellion where almost entire Bengal Army rebelled.

Till Indian army was loyal to the British, India could not become independent as army and police where the primary tool of enforcing British will using civil service.

Further as stated earlier, the German ruler Kaiser had offered support to Indian princes against the British. Gadar party had received support from outside India.

When Bose was released in December 1940, he put the plan in motion and escaped in January '41 even when his house was watched 24x7. Following a difficult route via Peshawar, Kabul and the Soviet Union reached Germany on an Italian passport under the name Orlando Marzzotta[13].

The exile of 1932 and stay in Europe had made him familiar with Europe; he had met Mussolini and his son-in-law Count Ciano earlier, and Bose spoke German. He had also met Himmler and Goering, the Nazi leaders during the exile.Being given a passport in the name of an Italian Embassy official was to avoid catching the eye of British intelligence which was very active in Kabul.

Within a week of reaching Germany in the first week of April '41, he put up demands to Germans that are remarkable in clarity and show that he had given the matter considerable thought even when he was in India:

Bose sent a lengthy memorandum to the German Foreign Office titled 'A plan for cooperation between Axis powers and India.'

---

[13.] Orlando Marzzotta was an employee of Italian Embassy in Kabul.

The Memorandum suggested setting up a Free India Government in Berlin and concluding a treaty between this Government and the Axis powers promising freedom to India. It also outlined a plan for propaganda and subversion in Afghanistan and the tribal areas of the Northwest frontier and for the rest of India.

Bose asked for the main base to be established in Afghanistan. Axis powers should send 50,000 soldiers to drive out the 70,000 British soldiers from the Indian subcontinent.'[88]

'The first position in the plan was recognition of a 'Free Indian government.' Woermann [14] accepted the plan with reservation and ruled out the formation of an Indian government in exile at this time. Neither did he approve a military expedition; however, he supported generous financial assistance.'[89]

The Germans were good hosts but reluctant supporters. It was only in January 1942 that Bose was able to start the India Independence League or Free India Center with twenty-five Indians who were screened by the German Foreign Office.

In January '42, Bose, who had so far been using the name Orlando Marzzotta, decided to reveal himself- held a function and disclosed his identity. Radio broadcasts were made in multiple languages to Indians from a transmitter located in Holland, and the service was named Azad Hind Radio and National Congress Radio. A team took care of these in multiple languages.

He created an Indian National Army from Indians who had become prisoners of War in Europe and Africa. Some joined, but many did not. The administrative issues with Germans persisted about whom they would fight and when because Bose insisted that the I.N.A. only fight

---

14. Of German foreign office

against the British to liberate India. Three thousand seven hundred joined I.N.A. There were multiple frictions with the Germans at every step, be it training /designations/oath/armaments, etc.

By this time, the war had gone differently than the initial German plans. Bose was continuously making an effort but, with inadequate developments in Germany, decided to go to Southeast Asia, where Japan had made huge victories over the British and which offered a land route via Burma to India.

Bose said: *'General Tojo, the Prime Minister of Japan, has repeatedly asserted the slogan of 'India for Indians' and has also explained its significance. In our struggle to free ourselves from the bonds of slavery, Japan will give us full support and assistance...'*

Bose's repeated push to meet his demand finally led to a meeting with Hitler in May 1942 when Hitler said, as per notes of his chief interpreter:

'India was endlessly far from Germany. The only possibilities of communication with India were by land or air...In any case, the path would be only over the corpse of Russia...The defeat of their power (British) in East Asia would possibly lead to the collapse of the British Empire. Such a collapse would naturally mean a great relief for Germany and spare her blood loss.[90]

Hitler went on to tell Bose that he would facilitate his trip to East Asia. The Fuhrer advised against the air route and said he would place a submarine at his disposal for the sea journey, which would be much safer.[91]

It took nine months before Bose could leave Germany for Southeast Asia. Meanwhile, his broadcasts continued. These radio broadcasts were widely heard in India. A staff member of the B.B.C.

during these months on tour in India reported being upset that the enemy broadcasts and All India Radio were now much more favored by Indian listeners than B.B.C. The Usual question when an Indian buys a wireless set, I was told by big dealers in Bombay, is: Can I hear Germany and Japan on this?[92]

Speaking to Indian National Army in Europe, he said in June 1942:

*'Today we are taking the vow of independence under the National Flag. A time will come when you will salute this flag in the Red Fort. But remember that you will have to pay the price of freedom. Freedom can never be had by begging. It has to be got by force. Its price is blood.'*[93]

In February '43, Bose and Abid Hassan boarded a German Submarine U-180. On the way to Asia, it sank the British merchant ship *Corbis*, and eventually linked with a Japanese submarine I-29 near Madagascar. Bose and Hassan effected a daring mid-sea transfer via a dingy.

*Indian National Army in Southeast Asia:*

The Indians in Southeast Asia, as elsewhere, were nationalists and tried to do their best for India. In the past, in their own way, many had tried to contribute to the freedom effort.

When World War II started, and Siam, Malaya, and Burma came under Japanese influence, the efforts towards freedom increased, and many cities had Indian Independence League trying their best.

When Japan took over Siam, Fujiwara Iwaichi of Japanese intelligence reached out to Pritam Singh, leader of the India Independence League in Bangkok, as stated earlier.

Together they decided to reach Kadeh, where there had been initial feelers from a disgruntled British Indian Army Major – Major Mohan Singh of the 1/15 Punjab regiment.

On December 30[th,] Major Singh confirmed to Pritam Singh and Fujiwara his participation and thus I.N.A. was born.

The slogan suggested by the Japanese for the unit was Asia for Asiatics.'[94]

At this stage, Mohan Singh informed Fujiwara about Subhas Bose stating, '*that in most cases, people worshipped him like a God.*' Bose in Germany was informed about this formation.

They reached out to other soldiers, and initially, a group of 229 soldiers was formed, and it was called F. Kikan (Kikan = Office). They wore an armband with the letter F to indicate that they worked for Fujiwara.

'When the British surrendered in Singapore on February 17[th,] 1942, 40,000 troops under Colonel Hunt were told by him, 'Now you belong to the Japanese Army.' Colonel Fujiwara addressed the troops in Japanese, which was first translated into English and then into Hindi; he told them they would not be treated as prisoners but as brothers.'[95]

Major Mohan Singh announced the formation of an 'Indian National Army.'[96] The place was the India Center on Serangoon Road in Singapore. Here F. Kikan graduated to I.N.A.

'Mohan Singh wanted twelve infantry battalions in four regiments -a force of around 8000 men with support units of around 2000 more. The recruits that came forward were stripped of their old regimental distinctions and placed in new units called Azad, Nehru, and Gandhi.'[97].

Meanwhile, the various India Independence Leagues had been in contact with one another, and it was decided to hold a meeting in Tokyo and proceed further with Japanese support.

Unfortunately, the plane in which Pritam Singh and some others were flying crashed, and Rash Behari Bose, who was president of the Indian Independence League in Japan, chaired the meeting.

General Tojo said in his message to the Tokyo Conference:

*'The Japanese Empire is determined to go ahead with its mission of destruction of the Anglo -Saxon power and will not rest until that mission is fulfilled. I want to state frankly that the Japanese Government cannot remain indifferent to the fact that Britain is going to make India the base of its East Defense.'*[98]

*Meanwhile, with his substantial influence in Japanese circles, Rash Behari Bose secured a declaration that Japanese forces and administration, even though at war with British Empire whose subjects Indians were – would not treat properties, businesses, and Indians as enemies or confiscate their properties. This allowed Indians free movement and activities and did not damage them financially.*

This enabled Indians to fund the I.N. A. and Azad Hind Government liberally, including a few cases where the persons gave all their assets.

Rash Behari was appointed president of the entire region at the Tokyo conference. He had tirelessly worked for Indian freedom and, at this stage, was President of Hindu Mahasabha in Japan and was constantly in touch with Veer Savarkar on revolutionary activities.

Subsequently, a conference was held in Bangkok from June 15th, where many decisions were made. One was to appoint Mohan Singh as the general commanding officer. Another was to ask the Japanese Government that I.N.A. be treated equally as Japanese Soldiers. They asked that I.N.A. only fight the British for Indian Independence.

For Rash Behari, who had been tirelessly working for Indian freedom since decades, this was another major effort toward freedom for India. He had left India after an attack on Lord Hardinge, the Viceroy, and escaped to Japan. He had never stopped working for Indian freedom.

'In January 1915, dual attempts to attack British India were made with two ships, *Annie Larson* and *S.S. Maverick*. The motive was to ship eleven cartloads of arms at the cost of $140,000 from the coast of Mexico. The *Maverick* finally entered Indian Waters by September after months of being lost at sea. It was to attack the *Sundarbans*[15]. From here, revolutionaries in India, such as Rash Behari Bose and Jatindranath Mukherjee (famously known as Bagha[16] Jatin) were to assist the unrest in the United Provinces, Punjab, and Bengal. Jatin belonged to the Jugantar revolutionary group of Bengal. They armed themselves with fifty Mauser pistols and 46000 rounds of ammunition.'[99]

'Rash Behari Bose made another attempt by coordinating an armed ship to attack Andamans, free the prisoners and lead them to Burma with two other warships were to follow to carry out strikes. However, the British heavy Cruiser *H.M.S. Cornwall* sank the ship in the Andamans.[100]

Conflicts arose with Major Mohan Singh and his behavior. Some army officers did not like elevating himself to General and his lack of leadership. The Japanese, still committed to the project and support, started looking for another leader, and that is when Rash Behari asked them to reach out to Subhas Chandra Bose. However, the Japanese were uncomfortable with how it would play out and if it would generate conflict between both the Bose's, who were unrelated. After they received explicit assurances from both -each agreed to work under each other- it was decided to arrange for Subhas Bose to come to Southeast Asia.

Meanwhile, Rash Behari asked Mohan Singh to step down, who ended up issuing a dissolution order. However, with the appointment of other people, particularly Major General Bhonsle and Major General

---

[15.] Area in Bengal – heavily forested
[16.] Bagha=Tiger

Kiani, Rash Behari was able to retain part of the I.N.A. and begin the restructuring process.

The Japanese also got confirmation from individual soldiers that they would work under Subhas Bose, and efforts started to get him to come. But it took time, and as of December 31, 1942, Subhas Bose was still in Germany.

But he was able to reach Singapore in May '43, and that changed everything for India. He later created a provisional Free India- Azad Hind government, regularized the Indian National Army as its armed force, and made an administrative structure. *Nine Countries recognized this Government, and the Indian National Army fought the battles as an independent army -never under a Japanese officer. Since certain people make much out that they were under Japanese command -let us not forget that British, Australian, Canadian, and other armies were under U.S. command in WWII- so the typical assertion that I.N.A was a subordinate army of Japanese as made out by some is not correct.*

# CHAPTER 6

# TRADE TO RULE-BRITISH IN INDIA

The Quit India movement was the last freedom movement organized by the Congress Party and Gandhiji. The movement is projected in popular narrative to have generated long-term discontent and public protests. To review this with context, let us begin by reviewing the British rule itself.

## *Evolution:*

The British awareness of merchandise from India and its prices came about from an act of piracy. Sir Francis Drake, a pirate captain in 1595, operating under a letter of Marquee[17], captured five ships; among them was the Portuguese ship *St. Philip,* which had cargo and papers that explained the value and method of trading in India.

England of the time was a poor, agricultural nation, in conflict with itself and having excessive superstitions and disputes as well as religious conflicts.

'There were highwaymen on the roads, pirates on the river, vermin abundance in the clothing and beds. The common food was peas, vetches, fern roots, and even the bark of trees.'[101]

---

17. Letter issued by British Queen permitting piracy

'It was a nation so illiterate that many of its peers in parliament could neither read nor write.'[102]

The trade route to India was not known to the British earlier. The first to establish were Portuguese, but in 1598, a Dutch cartographer who was secretary to the Archbishop of Goa published them first in Dutch than in English, and the secret was out for Western countries.

The London spice trade was via the Ottoman Empire or the Dutch, who had been trading with the islands that constitute today's Indonesia.

In 1600, a group of merchants known as the Levant Company of London raised money from its associates and created a new company called the 'The Company of Merchants of London, trading into the East Indies. 'It was a joint stock company where many people invested money.

When the Charter came thru on December 31st, 1600, for fifteen years, Elizabeth I was the queen, and there was one important condition: the Company had to generate profit within two years; otherwise, it would lose its Charter. The first governor was Sir Thomas Smith. The Company was allowed to waive customs duty on the first four voyages.

Therefore, the objective was money to be made quickly, and it pursued the same vigorously.

The first few voyages to the Spice Islands did not generate the expected return, though they did generate a profit. The Company was now in business, but it needed better.

It turned attention to textiles, and that meant India.

India at this time had almost 25% of the global GDP and was the wealthiest country according to some and second richest according to some.

It also had an interesting political structure. Thousands of rulers governed small parts of India. Most were limited to a small area, and they were actively involved in managing the affairs. They sent a part of the revenue to another ruler who ruled a more extensive territory and was their guide or protector. Then, the share was passed on to the central ruler. Thus, the paramount ruler – the Mughals, in this case for north India – were overlords. Still, they themselves ruled only a tiny area directly themselves. They ruled over other Rajahs and Nawabs and gave them designations defining their revenue contribution and position in the Mughal army and their commitment to a certain number of soldiers for the army. The Mughal Ruler was thus called *Shahenshah,* i.e., ruler of the rulers.

The revenue of the individual states came from the share of land revenue and transit fees charged on goods that moved through it. Goods exported out of India were not charged the transit fee. A document called Dustak was allowed to be issued by the exporter to the local authority to avoid paying the duty. An order 'firman' was required from the Mughal ruler for this in case it transited through the areas under him, i.e., the areas where he was the overlord.

The initial effort of the British to get permission to establish an office – called a factory – in Mughal rule failed with vigorous opposition by the Portuguese, who had a significant influence in the court. The Portuguese were also to fight major battles with the British for control of the sea route to India, which was finally won by the British.

The first factory was established in Masulipatnam, which was under one of the constituents of the former Golkonda Kingdom, not the Mughals. In 1619, another was opened in Pullicat.

The British started the trade from India, which was to England as well as to Siam and today's Indonesia, taking Indian cotton there and bringing spices and silks from there.

They tried to bring British woolen cloth from England but found no takers in India. Hence in accordance with prevailing practice, they had to pay Indian suppliers in silver. Since silver was not produced in England, this was either obtained in trade from Europe or via piracy, as most of the silver was carried by ships from Latin America to Spain. Thus in 1615, the Company, now called the East India Company.[18] (EIC) had become the largest silver exporter from England. This led to problems for the Company. Under the theory of mercantilism prevailing at that time, the country's wealth was supposed to be based on gold and silver. East India Company brought textiles and other consumer products while exporting silver and gold, which generated ire.

Another crisis was faced in the 1635 period when possibly due to a famine in India with Shahjahan-the Mughal Ruler's massive taxation, the procurement of textiles suffered, and the Company had to cut its staff in London.

The British could get another place in 1639-40 -Madraspatnam -on lease and start a factory. Then, the Mughal governor of Surat allowed them to trade and establish a factory in Surat. At this time, Surat was the biggest port in India.

The British Crown had authorized a second company to trade with India, which took away the monopoly of the East India Company in 1635, and they sent several ships to India. However, the stronger East India Company was able to get the second Company to merge with EIC. It had to resort to buying influence with the Crown and other decision-

---

[18.] In Popular Slang, it was called 'the John Company.'

makers. It learned to continuously manage the relationship with the Crown and other influential voices.

By 1650, Indian products accounted for 15% of the total imports of England.

In 1661, the British Monarch Charles II married Catherine Braganza of Portugal. Bombay was given as dowry to Charles II, and East India Company bought this from the Crown. The British built another settlement here called Fort St George. The Company had started establishing permanent settlements and keeping small armies. A cathedral was also started here.

In 1690, the EIC obtained three villages on lease from the Mughal Governor of Bengal, renamed them Calcutta, and, within the city, created Fort Williams headquarters.

By this time, India had Dutch, Portuguese, and French all vying for trade.

The Company fought battles for control of trade from other Europeans and as well as started taking sides in fights for the throne internal to some kingdoms or among different kingdoms. All the Europeans had begun maintaining small armies with firearms brought from Europe, which were better than what India had at that time, and trained Indian soldiers in their style of warfare technique taught and guided by experienced veterans of battles in Europe and ensuring that regular, steady salary payments are made. Most Indian armies suffered from irregular payments at this time. The European conflicts among different nations spilled over to India.

Other challenges for the Company were the greed of its officers, who wanted to keep a large part of the profit for themselves, and competition from interlopers, who were private traders who did not have trading rights as assigned by the Crown.

The rise of the Marathas started with Chhatrapati Shivaji, who established a Kingdom in the late seventeenth century. British fought a sea battle with Shivaji's navy as well. The Mughal Aurangzeb was away from his capital in Agra for more than 25 years to try and subdue the Marathas but failed.

Many more opportunities were felt by the Company after 1707, when Aurangzeb died, and different factions at the Mughal court vied for influence among themselves. By this time, the Company was also clear that India had a well-defined revenue system, and that land revenue was typically the most significant contributor to a King's treasury, not the tax on trade.

Meanwhile, in England, during the period of 1720s, the rise in protectionism sentiments led to the import of printed Indian fabrics being banned, and only plain fabric or raw fabric was allowed to be imported, which gave rise to an extensive print and embellishment industry in England. The English, who had been wearing wool round the year, had shifted to comfortable cotton in a significant way for wearing as well as home goods.

In the 1740s, various warring princes of Karnataka sought British and French help. The military assistance was paid for by Indians assigning land revenue and taxation to the Company.[103]

In 1748 the Company received the port of Tanjore-Devikottai and an annuity in exchange for support to the Rajah of Tanjore.[104]

Spending almost 150 years in India, the British had become aware of the vast fortunes that Indian princes had, vast riches at every level, and the affluence level of people. Then Nadir Shah came and took so much money from India that three years of taxes in the entire country of Persia were waived off. The Mughal rule had been in steady decline since the early part of the 18th century. Marathas had extended their control to almost all parts of India except Bengal, which was still under a Mughal Governor, Avadh, and certain other areas.

When the Mughal governor, i.e., Nawab of Bengal, Alaverdi Khan, died in 1756, he was succeeded by his adopted very young grandnephew Siraj ud Daulah became governor.

Bengal producer of textiles as well as saltpeter was crucial for the East India Company. *Between 1726 and 1753, Bengal supplied more than 50 percent of the value of goods exported from Asia.*[105]

In arrogance to show the world how rich he was, Siraj arranged a public counting of his cash money.

The cash wealth was 680 million rupees which was about £85[19] million.[106]

'Within a year, he had alienated his grandfather's officials, his greatest zamindars, his prominent bankers, and all the European trading Companies.' Historian Moon says 'he had uncontrolled temper and tyrannical conduct. He is said to have stuck Jagat Seth, the leading Hindu banker in the face and threatened him with circumcision '.[107] (i.e., conversion to Islam)

That became the opportunity for the British, who started fortifying Fort William without approval, generated conflict with Siraj, and ensured they had the disgruntled people to support them on various grounds.

Siraj tried to stop the fortification and took those British at Fort William prisoners who had not managed to run away. The history narrated in general is that only 23 survived the next day after being locked in a small room out of 146 people. This was a British prison in Fort William. The incident is called the incident of the black hole. Siraj left the British goods in the fort without impounding them.

---

[19.] Today's value is approx. $16623.30 Million

Now the Bengal East India Company saw the entry of wily, ambitious Robert Clive, who described himself as a 'Master of tricks, chicanery, intrigues, politics, and the lord knows what.'[108], who moved from Madras with his boundless ambition.

The incident was sought as justification for the subsequent battle of Plassey by raising a demand of £ 2 million for losses in Calcutta. Even British historians express severe doubts about this narration of black hole as presently presented in Indian history. The next day after this so-called incident, nothing was said by the E.I.C. officer to the Nawab; 156 people could not fit in an 18ft x15 ft.[109] room, and there is no record of the names of the dead or, indeed, if these many people were left in the fort. Even the total number of British deaths in Calcutta that year are recorded as 56, and none from suffocation.[110]

The officials at Siraj's court were bribed and induced, and Mir Jaffer, his army commander, agreed to betray Siraj, which he did on June 23rd, 1757, in the battle of Plassey[20] by switching sides in mid-battle. The Battle of Plassey was a well-planned event. The English had brought in armed forces from Madras as well. This was no spur-of-the-moment response as made out in popular historic narration. Moreover, the battle took place in June 1757, while the incident of the Black Hole occurred in June 1756, one year earlier.

In his memoirs of the revolution, Watts, whom the Company accredited to Nawab's court, freely admits that he resorted to wholesale bribery of Nawab's officers, ministers, and supporters for the success of English intrigues.'[111]

As compensation for losses suffered, 'From Nawab's treasury, English community got £500,000[21], Hindu merchants were given £222,000,

---

20. The area was full of Palash trees and hence the name Plassey
21. Today's value is approx. $94.8M

Armenian merchants £77000, British Army and Navy £275000, and the Company got land taxes ceded to them with a further £275000 to members of the council.[112]

Altogether the British got in cash 72,71,666 Silver Rupees on July 6[th,] 1757. Says historian Orne *'Never before did the English nation at one time obtain such a prize in solid money.'*[113]

As commander in chief and council member, Clive got the lion's share of the money that went to the Company and the English community. His share from replacing the Nawab came to £ 234,000[22].[114]

Now came the regular British games. The new Nawab Mir Jaffer could not keep up with British demands and was soon replaced by his son-in-law Mir Kasim who had been Mir Jaffer's representative in negotiating with the British. Even during the nominal rule of Mir Jaffer, most of the decisions were taken by Robert Clive. A wag among his courtiers gave Mir Jaffar the wickedly apt nickname of 'Col. Clive's donkey' and it stuck to him till his death.[115]

When Mir Kasim replaced Mir Jaffer in the new agreement, the Company became a state for the first time.

'Revenue of three districts of Bengal, Burdwan, Chittagong, and Midnapore, went to the Company besides at least £ 200,000 in cash. The Company was allowed to mint silver and gold coins.[116]

But Mir Kasim could not satisfy the greed of EIC either. So, Mir Jaffer, who had been living in Calcutta in exile, was brought back.

Soon Mir Kasim approached the Mughal ruler for help in reinstatement, and a direct conflict occurred between the British and Mughal ruler Shah Alam, who was supported by Avadh Armies. Shah

---

22. Today's value is approx. $44.59 Million

Alam betrayed his own side in the middle of the battle and later entered into a tripartite agreement with the British. Shuja, the Avadh ruler, paid Rs. 2.5 million in cash, agreed to pay the same every year, and gave up the city of Allahabad, which became the fourth big City after Calcutta, Bombay, and Madras in British control. Mir Jaffer remained the Nawab.

Mir Jaffer died in 1765, and the British deposed his second son, who had become Nawab.

In this treaty of Allahabad on August 9th, 1765, the Mughal signed over the Diwani (governorship)of Bengal, Bihar, and Orissa to the Company in exchange for £272,000 per year.[117]

The annual receipt of this territory was estimated to be £ 33 million[23] a year.[118]

Thus, the British accomplished many things. Governorship of the wealthiest province of India of the time, ruling a land area more extensive and more populous than Britain. The Bengal of that time was today's Bangladesh+ Indian West Bengal + present-day Bihar and Orissa.

The transition from trade to State had happened, opening floodgates for money extraction.

Immediately the British changed the revenue recovery system. As pointed out earlier, the remittance of revenue to the ruler was a small part of the total revenue collected, with a large portion retained locally. Even under the oppressive Mughal rule, only 10-15% of the total revenue was sent to the central ruler.

Now, the British asked for most of the money to be remitted to them, leaving hardly anything with the local area. It led to a decline in law and order, deterioration in local infrastructure, and so on. The

---

[23] Today's Value Approx. $6079 M

land rent was raised to around fifty percent, a rise of about four times the previous level, and large-scale torture was used to extract this as the amount was very high, and peasants could not afford the same and started abandoning the cultivated area.

The British model now was to stop bringing silver from England, use local revenue for purchasing goods for exports, and use the balance to pay salaries to the Englishmen here and local sepoys. The London office kept the entire proceeds from selling goods imported from India. Therefore, the Company In England became a giant cash cow. An accounting entry called 'Home Charges' was invented to balance the books. The money drain from India was massive. The precise details of the transactions were kept limited to the top key people. Therefore, the matter did not become widely known.

The employees of East India Company made fortunes in a few years. These were the results of commissions, misuse of Dastak, and later bribes from local princes. By this time, getting a job in India guaranteed a fortune. However, many people died in the long travel due to journeys in wind-driven ships and weather adaptability issues in India.

*'The impact of money taken from India was, to quote Macaulay,' they inflated the price of everything from fresh Eggs to rotten boroughs. The deluge of Gold Mohurs shaken from the Pagoda[24] tree dazzled the whole world.'*[119]

The British expelled the French from Bengal and monopolized the trade.

In 1768 Bengal came up under a famine due to: raising the rates of land rent, people running away from cultivation, and abandoning

---

[24.] Pagoda was an Indian Gold Coin equal to three silver rupees

the land hence reducing production and heavy taxation on everyday products like salt, tobacco, and such.

The price of rice went up six times. The general population could not afford it, but the British bought enough for themselves and their soldiers.

In their overpowering greed for personal wealth, the English employees of the Company, high and low, had now thrown overboard the distinction between right and wrong and the Company's interests. They openly resorted to freebooting, which they carried on[120]:

'With impunity in Bengal and elsewhere… the counting-house was deserted continually for marauding expeditions; during this period, the business of a servant of the Company was simply to wring out of the natives a hundred or two hundred thousand pounds as speedily as possible, that he might return home.'[121]

The estimates of famine deaths vary, but the widely accepted figure is that one-third population died.

The torture methods are too gruesome to be detailed here. Still, they can be read in *William Howitt's* book -*The English in India- published in 1839*-in pages 65 to 68, which includes beating and flogging of men, raping young girls, and pulling off nipples from women.

Meanwhile, after the Bengal acquisition, the parent company in London was in an expansive mode. It increased its dividend first from 6 to 10%, then to 12 ½% and agreed to pay £400,000 yearly to the Crown. After the takeover of Bengal and with the income increase, everyone in England connected with EIC was in a joyous mood.

The impact of famine, loss of productive workforce, and consequent loss of revenue, together with the most share of revenue being kept by the Company's employees, ensured that the EIC in London had a cash flow crisis and came close to bankruptcy in 1773. When the Crown bailed it out, it put it under management control, and the top representative in India, now called the Governor-General, had to be nominated by the British Crown. The Company was given a new charter under the Act of 1773.

E.I.C. also acted as a banker, which increased the cash crisis and brought out the substantial private wealth generated in the open. An employee could give the money in India, collect a promissory note, and collect cash against this in England after paying a small fee. It added to cash money in India in hand but took it out of the Company's hands in England from its generous cash flow.

The obscene profits were being made by individuals deputed to India who used every trick in the book – commissions on purchase, commissions on freight – bribes for Dustak, and plundering the people. These amounts, however, became so large that these impacted the cashflow and profitability of the London office.

The British society was beginning to express concerns as some, after accumulating wealth in India, tried to buy estates, etc., in England and upset other aristocracies besides the feeling of jealousy.

These British guys who had made fortunes in India were called Nabobs – a variation on Nawab and were projected as immoral, corrupt, and philanderers.

When allegations were made, Robert Clive was investigated, but though his vast fortune was recognized, he was inexplicably given a clean chit.

The Governor Generals were now selected with the intent to curb corruption and secure the fortunes of the Company instead of just its employees. The Company was also planning for a long-term presence.

Warren Hastings, the first Governor General, tried to study Ramayana and Mahabharata and understand Hindus. He also established the Asiatic Society of Bengal for this purpose. The purpose was to get a better understanding of the natives.

When the next Governor General Lord Cornwallis -who had been sent after his having lost the final battle in the United States to General George Washington – and thus was responsible for losing the United States, he instituted many changes in Bengal to ensure that the British could keep Bengal under slavery. A Zamindar-based revenue system was created. A British judge decided the litigation – in the process, providing thousands of jobs to the British unemployed as lawyers and created a paternalistic culture giving first preference to Britons.

Cornwallis, by instituting the Zamindari system, destroyed the local welfare system. The hereditary grants to the temples acted as a social shock absorber by ensuring that no one slept on an empty stomach and that doing work would get enough for basic needs. The temples, in most cases, had a Gurukul[25], and most of the society thus was educated.

He broke the treaty with the Mughal ruler on payment of revenue. He made Avadh a subordinate state extracting money. He replaced the Benares ruler as the earlier ruler was unwilling to pay the sum demanded by the Company.

He deputed Indian sepoys for the first time overseas, a practice that continued till 1947.

Cornwallis also changed the administrative system to keep law and order by creating police stations and assigning specific territory to the chief of that police station with vast powers. Called 'Daroga,' they became

---

[25.] School

a terror in their own right due to powers, extracting money from people, and creating a favor-based environment.

In 1773, the Company imposed a monopoly on the opium trade. The opium had been actively promoted in China to replace making payment in silver to the Chinese from whom tea was being imported in England in such large quantities that the British economy was threatened. The best opium was grown in Bihar, now under the East India Company. Then, these were exported to China, where the East India Company sold to mostly British merchants on open seas as the opium trade in China was illegal. The merchants gave opium to the Chinese merchants and bought tea, which was then shipped globally.

East India Company thus had become the world's first multinational drug lord.

Some of the leading Hong Kong business houses of today trace their inception and fortune to opium.

Weavers in Bengal were forced to accept a little money as earnest money from the Company towards the orders. Later, this was used to ensure that they could not make goods for anyone else and were put into virtual slavery for the rest of their life.

The Company was the ruler, revenue collector, and trader all in one.

Meanwhile, the expansionist policies of the Company brought them into conflict with Marathas, whose four generals, Scindia (Shinde), Gaikwad, Holkar, and Bhonsle, had established principalities. Though technically they were under Peshwa, but in practice, they functioned independently and also had much intrigue.

The British inserted themselves into Peshwa politics and the courts of others by using devious methods like bribes, blackmail, and selective armed support; they were becoming a key influence.

The Major change in territory held by the British in India came when Richard Colley, later titled Marquis Wellesley, was sent as Governor-General. He was ambitious, and he insisted on a group of six officials to accompany him – two of whom were his brothers, including Arthur Wellesley, who became famous in history later as Duke of Wellington after the battle of Waterloo with Napoleon.

Wellesley said before leaving for India: *'I will heap kingdoms upon kingdoms, victory over victory, revenue upon revenue. I will accumulate glory and wealth and power until the ambition and avarice even of my masters shall cry mercy'.*[122].

He accomplished much during his tenure. With the six key people whom he had brought with him- his significant advantage was that his instructions were followed, and he could thus follow a strategy as well as execute it. At this time, the various officers of the Company in different locations were frequently at loggerheads with each other. With correspondence taking a few days or a week or two, it was possible to explain away non-compliance with a directive.

The big fear the British had at this time was the ambition of Napoleon, who wanted to be in India and was therefore seeking opportunities. The Wellesley efforts started by subduing Nizam first, taking him away from the French and ensuring he would not come to Tipu's aid. Tipu was trying to get help from Ottomans in Turkey. He had made extensive armament purchases in France, and his army was trained by the French. He had tried to hire mercenaries from other Muslim lands to support him. Tipu's father was the army chief of the Mysore kingdom and had usurped the Crown by displacing the Rajah. Tipu is known in history for his forcible imposition of religion, plunder of wealth of temples, and savagery. He had even tried to change the names of various places, methods of keeping time, and renaming weights and measures.

After once being defeated by Tipu in the period before the arrival of Wellesley in the first Mysore war, the British had secured a significant win in the third Mysore war in 1790 when they grabbed half of his territory, and Tipu had to leave his two sons as a hostage till he paid the money demand of the British.

In the fight with the British, when Governor-General Wellesley was in charge of India, Tipu was killed. After giving a small part of the territory to Nizam, who had helped them, the British kept a large part for them. Then, they reinstated a descendant of the Mysore Rajah with a small territory. Tipu's descendants were taken to Calcutta and lived life under British supervision. Says Penderel Moon, 'He was not an Indian patriot or nationalist in the modern sense. He was, first and foremost, a bigoted Muslim. Though he employed Hindus in his service, he regarded them all with some contempt as infidels.'[123]

Tipu had built a vast fortune by robbing temples, raising taxes, and collecting it brutally. Apart from what the soldiers plundered, the value of bullion, jewels, arms, and stores captured at Seringapatam amount to about £ 2M shared between EIC and army officers.[124]

Wellesley changed the Company forever. His team fought battles all around. Grabbed part of the territory from Scindia, won Delhi and Agra after displacing Scindia, the Mughal ruler's protector at that time. Thus, he finished Mughal rule in India and reduced the Mughal ruler to a pensioner of the Company. In the treat of Surji-Anjangaon Mughals were allowed to live in the Red Fort of Delhi. He was allotted a tiny area of Delhi for revenue that sustained him in the future. The year was 1804. The Mughal rule of India was over for all practical purposes.

The Wellesley period is therefore known for its expansion, removing the French threat to the British, subduing Nizam, removal of Tipu, finishing Mughal rule of India and making the Mughal ruler a British subject, and taking away forts and territories from Maratha rulers. Peshawa Bajirao II was put on the throne with British help in 1803. Scindia lost Ahmednagar in the same year, followed by the entire area of Gujarat and parts of Maharashtra. Bhonsle territories of Orissa and Jagannathpuri were occupied in 1803, and in 1805, finally, the British could overcome the considerable resistance of the Raja of Bharatpur. Avadh annexation was done in 1801.

By the time Wellesley returned to Britain after spending seven years in India, the British had established an Empire. It was no longer limited to the Cities of Bombay/Madras and the State of Bengal. It extended all over India. Besides, the 'subsidiary alliance' arrangements had been entered with many princes. Though Wellesley had accomplished his goal of raising 'an insignificant trading settlement to a mighty empire,[125] the Marathas were still unwilling to accept British domination quickly and quietly.

In the next twenty years, multiple wars had to be fought with Marathas by the British, which enabled them to establish British hegemony in India. The wars resulted in the severe curtailment of Maratha territory. They were won by the British only by a combination of deceit, trickery, bribery, and superior war strategy, which included generating friction among Marathas, creating misunderstanding, and taking up the fight with each one separately and after putting them into a situation where they could not call others for help.

The Marathas were not complicit or totally subservient to the British, as is made out many times. Savage battles were fought, and they did not give up easily. However, they could not match the British strategy in wile and bribing their ministers.

When Scindia finally made the agreement with the British, Arthur Wellesley wrote to Major Shaw, private secretary to his elder brother Governor-General Wellesley:

*'We have got such a hold in his Durbar that if ever he goes to war with the Company, one-half of his chiefs and his army will be on our side.'*[126]

Wellesley had been called back as he and his team had rubbed up other British officials in India, and the Company had sacrificed short-term profits due to massive expenditure in all the wars. Still, the long-term beneficial impact on East India Company was not immediately understood in London.

The British now had an Empire, but Wellesley was not given recognition for this till 1836. *Marquess Wellesley augmented his family's achievement by adding a line from the Aeneid' Super Indos protenit Imperium' (He extended the empire over the Indians).*[127]

The subsidiary alliance under which a Senior British official was placed in the native prince's kingdom with a team of British officials and a sepoy army was able to start controlling the princes with the unwritten threat of displacement in the event of the displeasure of the British.

In 1813, the Charter had again come up for renewal. With the gains the British had made now, the Evangelicals wanted the spread of Christianity as a goal to be added as well.

In the next few decades, the British fought wars with Nepal, Displaced and ended Peshwa's rule, and by the end of the third Maratha wars had curtailed Maratha power severely.

Fights with Nepal, dubbed Gurkha Wars, expanded British rule to Shimla and Mussoorie in the Himalayas, which later became significant British summer spots.

The Burma wars in 1825-26 finally resulted in the Treaty of Yanbo, where a treaty similar to a subsidiary alliance was signed, an indemnity was paid to the British, and part of the territory was given to the British.

The opium trade was encouraged and pushed. By the 1820s, opium was the single largest export item of the East India Company. It accounted for 15% of the revenue of the Company.

After the conquests in this phase, planning and effort started to *rule India forever*. After all, this was a tap that not only generated money and resources but sepoys taken from India also allowed the British to expand elsewhere and maintain control. Mid-level Indian administrators and shopkeepers were helpful from Hong Kong to Fiji to West Indies besides Africa.

When the Charter of the Company was renewed in 1833, the merchants in Hong Kong had become very powerful in the parliament. Instead of depending upon the East India Company, they wanted direct links with Indian trading houses to procure opium.

The East India Company lost its trading privilege. It was made into a state with the power to enact laws, mint currency, appointed officials, etc.

The Governor General of Bengal was now redesignated as the Governor General of India.

In the 1830s, the steamship had become the usual mode of transport between India and England, which reduced the travel time from anywhere between 4-6 months and dependence upon winds to 25-30 days depending upon season and minimizing the impact of weather. This also made ships larger and journeys comfortable, resulting in a large influx of women. Previously, there were hardly any women coming to India, resulting in a large number of Anglo-Indian children from Indian wives or mistresses, besides huge issues of prostitution and venereal diseases. The point of prostitution and mistresses was reduced in upper segments of British society in India; however, it continued in other segments as British women were not enough to accommodate many British soldiers.

The avarice continued unabated. There were Afghan Wars in the 1840s when expansion was sought into Afghanistan. When Lord Dalhousie became Governor General, he tried to put many controls and conditions on princes, which enabled him to take over and merge many Kingdoms in British-ruled India. The only princely State where the British honored their agreement was Punjab as long as Maharaja Ranjit Singh was alive. After his death, his son was forced to give the world-famous Kohinoor as a gift. The son was taken to England and converted to Christianity. Punjab became part of British-ruled India.

The extraction of money on any and all pretexts continued. The State interfered to collect tax on almost everything. An example of the period is the Stamp Act, which required all official documents to be put on stamp paper whose revenue went to the State.

The reeducation program of Indians was started under a policy instituted by Macaulay to produce clerks and support staff for the British ruling class. Various religious groups freely established These schools and colleges and reserved seats for those who had converted to Christianity. As knowing English was essential for jobs in British organizations, services, and law courts, it became necessary to study in these colleges for Indians who wanted to improve their status in life.

Plans were made for bringing railways to India to achieve faster and more secure transport for goods to the port. This provided jobs and opportunities for England's industrialization and cargo for British steamship companies. The bonds were issued, which paid high returns to investors. Everything was imported from rails, Engines to compartments. The freight rates were kept low, and the passenger traffic from the lowest class-third class subsidized the 1st class, whose fares were high, but the number of passengers carried was much lower. So, if yield per compartment is calculated, the 1st class yielded much less than a 3rd class compartment.

In the next fifty years, the railway network was expanded as required by the freight and then focused on moving the army as quickly as may be needed.

By the late 1850s, the princes were upset with the Dalhousie Doctrine on inheritance; the public was upset due to high taxation and massive religious conversion efforts. Then the trigger came in 1857 when both Hindus and Muslims got upset simultaneously due to cartridges that had to be opened by mouth and were rumored to be greased with beef tallow and lard of Pigs. The Cows are sacred to Hindus, and Pigs are dirty to Muslims. Both treated this as an assault on their religious practices and attempts to convert.

A rebellion started in a military barrack and soon extended to many parts of the country. Though the rebel leaders went to Delhi to ask Bahadur Shah, the old and feeble Mughal, to rule, he had not done anything that required leadership in his lifetime. The only life he knew was of nautch, women, and entertainment. Ultimately, the rebellion, which Indians call the first War of Independence, was put down very savagely. In many cases, the soldiers were tied to the mouths of the canon and blown up.

The British Crown decided to take over the administration of India from the East India Company, and Queen Victoria became the Empress of India in 1858.

CHAPTER 7

# RULE VIA LEGAL SHACKLES

The suppression of 1857 could be done by British with all available resources being pitched in including troops from Britain. There were three separate armies of the East India Company under each presidency. The Bengal army was almost fully demobilized, which had led the fight for independence.

Parts of the Madras and Bombay armies were also demobilized. The British were uncomfortable with the castes and sub-groups who had given them a tough fight while trying to expand the empire. So, their biggest dissatisfaction was with those who were part of the Maratha armies.

'It was an axiom of the Company's policy reemphasized by the mutiny that India was ruled by force of arms. The shock of the Mutiny and the degree of success achieved by the mutineers imposed an enduring pattern of development on army administration. The British element was increased, and the sepoy element diminished till a rough proportion of one to two was reached. This was maintained right down to 1914. Further, the artillery was placed in British hands, and sepoy battalions were recruited on a potentially less explosive, mixed basis of class and caste. Later in the century, the Russian threat encouraged the policy of recruiting from those people, in particular the Gurkhas, Pathans, and Sikhs, who had shown a warlike talent.'[128]

The annual cost of the army, borne entirely on Indian revenues, was heavy, amounting in the 1880's for example, to some 50 crore rupees and absorbing about one-third of the Government's budget.[129]

'In the Bengal Army, the Grenadiers of the line was popular enough, and for long, the Bengal Army was almost entirely composed of the tall Hindustani sepoys from Oudh and Behar, Rajput's and actual Brahmins, the Oudh Brahmin making a fine soldier or Moslems of the same provinces either Turks and men of Afghan origin or Sheikh's men of good clans who had been converted.'[130]

Says MacMunn, With the reconstruction which gave to the Punjabi, the military birthright hitherto accorded to the Hindustani [26],the classes from whom the new Bengal Army was to be drawn were:

1.  Tribesmen from the N.W. Frontier both within and without the border.

2.  The cultivating classes from the Punjab plain Viz. Sikhs, Muhammadans, and Hindu Rajputs from the Punjab Hills are known as Dogra.

3.  Certain of the classes of Hindustan are listed in the old army but to a far lesser extent.

4.  Men of Nepal and the adjoining hills Viz. Gurkhas, Garhwalis, Kumauni's.

5.  The Madras and Bombay Armies as before, the former with its Tamil and Telegu peasantry, its pariah classes and Christians, and the Moslem descendants of Afghan, Turk, and Arab settlers. The

---

[26] The word at that time meant North India Bengal to U.P in British colloquial language

Latter with its Mahrattas and Dekhani Moslems of descent similar to those in Madras.[131]

The method of governance and system of control of the population changed. The British now ruled by imposing obnoxious laws via the 'steel structure'[27] of Civil service and enforcing the will via 'Sword,' i.e., a Police force or British Indian Army.

Under the Government of India Act of 1858, the governance of India shifted to a council of 15 persons who advised the Governor General. - now redesignated as Viceroy. Among the significant promises made was perpetual nonintervention in matters of religious belief or worship in British India, i.e., Not enforcing forced conversions to Christianity and reversal of the aggressive policy of annexation of Lord Dalhousie, leaving the princes to decide on the issues of succession and adaptation as long as they swore undying allegiance to the British Crown.

At the same time, to avoid princes being against the British and have them align their loyalties towards the British, they were sought to be educated in a college, especially for aristocrats in India -Mayo College in Ajmer and Doon School in Dehradun besides Eton and similar in England and then subsequently higher education in England and encouraged to lead a life of luxury, sports and away from governance.

The British learned from 1857 not to oppress both Hindus and Muslims simultaneously and divided the society, and played favorites.

Under East India, officials were inducted into service by a nomination by directors; the administration of India was changed via a competitive examination and governed by the Indian Civil Services Act of 1861.

---

[27] As described by Lloyd George, the British Prime Minister

Further, society was put under shackles. So many new laws were made that at the slightest discomfort, the police could arrest a person, and the justice system was such that it may take a perfectly innocent person years to clear the name, destroying mental sanity and financial well-being besides the impact on the family.

Some of these laws were:

Criminal Tribes Act: In this, certain communities were defined as criminal, their movements were restricted to a specific area, and employment opportunities were limited. Later most of them were declared as backward and classified as depressed classes after having spent decades in this category. The blame for this being depressed was placed on Caste Hindus.

The Arms Act: severely limited the ability to keep arms. The license was required, which was issued with great difficulty and only to pro-British people. The impact was that an armed rebellion was now largely impossible, and even when revolutionaries tried to obtain firearms, they were mostly discovered in the acquisition process.

Laws were made to regulate prostitution for the convenience of British soldiers, and places called Chakla were created with broad power to classify any girl as prostitute and put in Chakla.

Indian Penal Code of 1860 defined the various acts that could invite the law.

The Sedition Act of 1870 put stringent controls on criticism of rulers and actions.

Even something like The Factories act promulgated in 1881 puts imprisonment and fines on owners /occupiers for the tiniest of violations, such as failure of a factory to display provisions of the factories act adequately.

The country carried on tied with these harsh shackles, but the spirit of freedom was not dead, and innovative expressions were found. An I.C.S. officer Bankim Chandra Chattopadhyay wrote a novel *Anand Math* whose song *Vande Mataram*[28] was to become the swan song of freedom fighters.

The policy of divide and rule was put in full play. The census started recording separate religions and sects and went to extremes to record facial features.

When the Mughals ruled India, they encouraged Muslims from other countries who came here by allotting key administrative and army positions. These were designated as Ashraf and constituted Turks from Turkey, Pathans from Afghanistan and Tajikistan, Iranians, etc. These were given priority by the British also- because most of the Islamic thought leaders came from these segments as well as they controlled Islamic Clergy.

'The British classified Muslims Sheikh, Sayyad, Mughal, Mirza, Mallik, and Pathan, who were considered Ashraf, i.e., nobly born and Ajlaf (lower class) and Arlafs. (Degraded class[29]). Ajlaf and Arlafs are converted from Hindus.'[132]

Ashraf group was sought to be encouraged by distancing from Hindus. Sir Syed Ahmed Khan was assisted in forming Anglo-Oriental College in 1875 in Aligarh (which eventually became Aligarh Muslim University).

Sir Penderel Moon, who has written two voluminous books on India and was in Civil Service during the partition period in India, quotes the statement of Sir Syed in 1888 'India is a country inhabited by two different nations, and there would necessarily be a struggle for

---

[28] Vande Mataram, I bow to the mother. In this case Mother India. Link to the original song https://www.youtube.com/watch?v=xj1Iy4nRMkc

[29] These terms are offensive but retained as per original text.

power between them if the English were to leave. Is it possible that under these circumstances, two nations – the Mohammedan and Hindu could sit on the same throne and remain equal in power? Most certainly not. It is necessary that one of them should conquer the other and thrust it down. To hope that both could remain equal is to desire the impossible and inconceivable.[133]

While these forces were being encouraged, three other significant events took place during this period:

In 1867, Darul-Uloom, soon to develop into one of the world's most important centers of Islamic thought, was established in Deoband[30], which printed curricula, produced legal opinions, issued fatwas, i.e., authoritative opinions on legal matters, and created a 'government within a government.'[134] The followers of their thoughts are called Deobandi within the Islamic fold.

Barelvi's school of thought was started by Ahmed Khan Reza Barelvi in the 1880s, which also influenced Muslim thinking, and later they had a hard-liner attitude towards Indian Independence, supporting Mohammed Ali Jinnah and Muhammad Iqbal.[135].

The third was the formation of the Indian National Congress by A.O. Hume, a retired British I.C.S. officer. He formed the party inviting like-minded British officials and educated Indians, and most of the people who joined him early on were lawyers.

As per records of the Congress party, the motivation for Hume in formation was as below:

People prayed for but despaired of getting:

'a.   justice cheap, sure, and speedy

b.   Police they could look up to as friends and protectors,

---

[30.]   A city In United Provinces (U.P.).

c.   A land revenue system more elastic and sympathetic and

d.   A less harsh administration of the arms and forest laws.'[136]

'He was inspired to intervene as:

'Mr. Hume had unimpeachable evidence that the political discontent was going underground. He came into possession of seven volumes containing reports of the seething revolt incubating in various districts of various gurus to their religious heads… Not that an organized mutiny was ahead but that the people, pervaded with a sense of hopelessness, wanted to do something by which was merely meant 'a sudden violent outbreak of sporadic crime, murders of obnoxious persons, robbery of bankers and looting of bazaars acts really of lawlessness which by a due coalescence of forces might any day develop into a National revolt.'[137]

*'Hume thereupon resolved to open a safety valve for this unrest, and the Congress was such an outlet.'*[138]

Congress party, therefore, became a conduit for channeling educated Indian public opinion to the British. All copies of their resolutions were also sent to the Viceroy for the first 20 years or so.

Later it was to become a forum for Indians to express themselves. Therefore, it had people from various ideologies, ranging from the extreme left, i.e., socialist leaning, to the moderate and extreme right, who preferred revolutionary and more aggressive methods like Chittranjan Das.

By the time the early 20th Century came in, India was in flux. The Partition of Bengal, based on religious lines that Eastern Bengal had a Muslim majority and Western Bengal had a Hindu Majority, aroused strong feelings. Another conflict was that Eastern Bengal was the major producer of raw materials processed in Western Bengal.

This partition was taken back after vigorous protests.

The British created a horrible penal prison in Andaman and Nicobar Island. 'The prisoners here were subjected to a punishing labor regime, starved, tossed into solitary for months at a time, deprived of the most basic hygiene, and tortured with mechanical devices, among other persecutions. '[139]

Usually, this was reserved for freedom fighters whose spirit was intended to be broken as well as serve as an example to others so the people do not fight for freedom. But they did, without bothering for their lives and hardships fight against the British was carried out by many young people. Some fought to avenge local injustice in specific cases, while others tried to make more significant efforts. Those who were caught went thru hell. Some, like Rash Behari Bose, were able to escape. He went to Japan after the attempt to kill Lord Hardinge, the Viceroy, went wrong.

Gadar party started operating from the West Coast of the United States and Canada towards freedom for India. However, the British were able to infiltrate their network and ensured that Canada and the United States tried and punished them, thus ending this effort.

The resource extraction from India continued unabated. Said Dadabhoy Naoroji:

'Britain's *drain of wealth was far worse than the plunder of India by Mahmud of Ghazni or Nader Shah. Its most important effect, Naoroji argued, was to deprive India of the resources needed to maintain its resilience in different conditions and grow. India was 'depleted," exhausted,' and 'bled,' so Indians found themselves pushed to the edge of subsistence when flood or drought came. The drain meant that there was a continuous 'chronic state of famine.'* [140]

This observation is from when wealth transfer methods and most documents were kept confidential and not disclosed to Indians. In Naoroji's calculations, this massive drainage amounted to about £12 million per year, while William Digby calculated it to be £30 million. On average, this accounted for at least half of the total revenue income of the British Indian Government.[141]

While the jobs allotted to Indians were at the lowest end of the spectrum, the jobs which were exclusive prerogative or had mainly British paid outrageously high salaries, making this as another form of exploitation.

The viceroy was Rs. 250,000 per annum plus liberal allowances, the Commander in Chief at 100,000 per annum plus allowances, and some of the secretaries to the Government of India who were I.C.S. officers at 48,000 per annum. The Government of India also paid salaries to the Christian Clergy- so Bishop of Calcutta was at 45,977 and Bishops of Madras and Bombay at 25,000[142].

To compare, this was the time when gold was Rs. 16.55 per ten grams.[143]

The British had attempted to divide Indians along religious lines, caste lines, social group lines, and so on. Every single imaginable division was sought to be introduced.

In the census, they classified separate religions existing in India as below:

Separate religious groups: Animism/Animism passing into Hinduism/Hinduism/Sikhism/Jainism/Buddhism/Zoroastrianism/Muhammadanism/Christianity/Judaism.

'They identified seven classes of Hindus and bifurcated the people.

Besides Identified separate groups, some of whom are given below which the British could not put strictly in the four caste classifications:

Khatri/Kayastha/Rajput/Nayyar/Lodha/Kurmi/Maratha/Meo…

The British also attempted to categorize people based on Tribal affiliations/Languages /Migration patterns/Looks of people.'[144]

Historian Elkins summarizes India of the time as follows '*Thus, the initial acts of conquest gave way in the twentieth Century to elaborate legal codes and the proliferation of police and security forces. Free market and labor controls for the colonized and administrative apparatuses that marginalized and oppressed entire populations while fueling racial and ethnic divisions within and between them.*[145]

*3 Allowing a little say:*

As the twentieth Century progressed, the impact of divide and rule and other British policies began to emerge in a much sharper manner.

'A delegation of Muslim leaders under the leadership of Aga Khan under the aegis of All India Muhammedan Deputation met Lord Minto in 1906, the Viceroy, and received favorable reception for their demands of separate electorates for Muslims in any scheme of political reform on the ground that they were loath to place 'our national interest at the mercy of an unsympathetic majority. At the same time, it asked for a due share for them in the gazetted and the subordinate and ministerial service.'[146]

The other demands ranged from representation in the executive council, fellows of universities, Nominations in the provincial council, nomination in the Viceroy's council, municipal representation, and so on. The delegation, which consisted of merchants, lawyers, etc., was from different subsects of Islam and regions of India.[147].

In 1906 Muslim League was formed in Dhaka to represent and insist upon the interests of Muslims. This organization claimed to represent all Muslims whom the British had divided into

Shia, Sunni, Ahmadiyya, Khoja, etc., besides Ashraf, Ajlaf, and Arlaf.

In 1909 the Marley- Minto reforms were sought to be implemented in India. These were to offer limited representatives to Indians in local governance. The act was to introduce elected representatives within various constraints as may be decided for local governments.

It also sought to create separate representatives for professional classes, the landholders, Muslims, Hindus, and European and Indian Christians. Particular property and other qualifications were laid down for being a voter, with levels for Muslims lower than for Hindus. Muslims were also given a higher weightage than the population.

As analysts believe this gave a huge fillip to the separatist movement and was to lead to a religion-based partition of India eventually.

In the beginning, it was opposed by Congress, but in 1916, a joint session of the Muslim League and Congress was held, and this was accepted.

Meanwhile, Hindu Mahasabha had been formed who opposed this.

Now onwards, whenever the issue of representation cropped up. Muslim League claimed to speak for all Muslims, and Congress was treated as speaking for Hindus. The reality was somewhat different. At that time Muslim League did not speak for all Muslims, and Congress claimed to represent both Muslims and Hindus. In fact, three of the Congress presidents in the 1910-30 period were past presidents of the Muslim League. Hindu Mahasabha tried to have a voice but was usually bypassed and ignored, and both the British and Congress did their best to throttle them.

By the Government of India Act of 1919, Separate electorates were made into a law.

The end of the world war brought its own challenges. The British Indian army had been increased with over a million men who fought outside India, and when they were back, Spanish Flu came back with them, which caused the death of almost twelve million people in India[148]. Besides, India was forced to gift England £100 million and buy £100 million in war Bonds which, taken together, was equal to four times the revenue of the Government of India at that time.

In first world war I, Indians under the arms for the British suffered 64000 dead and 67000 injured.[149]. More men were killed from India than from any other dominion.[150]

'The revolutionaries and freedom fighters (term in British texts: terrorists, anarchists) were in the minority, **but their activities were truly disturbing to the rulers'**[151].

'Around 1915, in Bengal alone, eight hundred orders were put into force that eviscerated civil and political liberties, such as they existed.'[152].

Congress party had become a forum for nationalist movements during this period. Though in the earlier period, Congress Presidents had bestowed lavish praise on the British; the needle had somewhat shifted though Congress continued to have a soft approach. The leaders of this time, Tilak, Gokhale, and Lala Lajpat Rai, had different views.

In 1915 Gandhiji came to India from South Africa. He had received much pre-arrival praise including from the Viceroy Lord Hardinge, who had praised his methods. Much about Gandhiji was lost in the fog, like the fact that the event of being thrown from the train was in 1893, and that did not create discontent with the British Empire as he fought as a Sergeant in British Army in the Boer war in 1908-1909.

When he came to India, he sought to enroll Indians for first world war I and received an award 'Kaiser -i-Hind 'from the British for his efforts. This was later returned under protest.

By 1920 path was clear for Gandhiji to take over the leadership of the Congress party. Gopal K Gokhale died in 1915, and Tilak, who had been pursuing Swaraj- Self Rule aggressively, died in 1920. He had stated, *'Home rule is my birthright, and I shall have it*[153] and worked towards it. Among his notable achievements is converting the Ganesh immersion procession to a huge nationalist procession, a practice that continues to date.

Justifying support to the British during World War I, later, Gandhiji wrote, ' If we would improve our status through the help and cooperation of the British, it was our duty to win their help by standing by them in their hour of need.'[154].

Praise from the British, massive favorable media coverage in English papers which then percolated down to language press, the launch of two newspapers by Gandhiji, 'Young India' in English and 'Navjivan' in Gujarati, and a carefully built persona as a Hindu saint allowed Gandhiji to dominate the narratives and the field quickly. The reality may have been different as Subhas Bose was to say, 'Mr. Gandhi emerged as a virtual dictator of the Congress.'[155]. People assigned mystic powers to him.

'The Imagined Gandhi was endowed with extraordinary occult power; peasants believed him to be a saint who could heal diseases. The rumors prevalent among the tribals of Bengal revealed their supreme faith in Gandhi's protective power; if they wore a Gandhi cap or chanted Gandhi's name, they believed police bullets could not harm them.'[156]

Now Gandhi's ideology became Congress ideology, and he pushed through a change to Congress policy.

'Congress in 1920 amended its constitution to declare the goal of the Congress to be swaraj (which literally means self-rule), and it was left to individual congressmen to define swaraj in their own way. Mr. Gandhi, however, defined swaraj as **'Self-government within the empire- if possible and outside if necessary.'**

Also, the constitution was changed so Congress could adopt all **peaceful and legitimate means.'**[157]

Congress policy now was changed to keep revolutionaries out as much as possible – though they had friction and could not get Subhas Bose out completely. But no revolutionary ever found support from Congress. Similarly, in the name of secularism, Congress permitted many leaders to be in the Muslim League and Congress simultaneously.[31].

Gandhiji had launched two Satyagraha. First in Champaran, Bihar. In Champaran, the issue was oppressive taxation and directed against Indigo landlords. The British suspended the unreasonable assessment.

Second, In Ahmedabad, there was a conflict between labor and mill owners, which was resolved by referring the matter to an arbitrator.

This gave the impression to the country that this was a viable method to resolve the disputes.

In Gandhiji's belief 'The ideology of Satyagraha was a spiritual state achieved by a man or woman, which gave them the inner fortitude, patience, and faith in God that was needed for passive resistance against an immoral authority. The degrees of physical suffering that the

---

[31.] Three leading members common were Hakim Ajmal Khan, Mohammed Ali Jauhar, and Mukhtar Ahmed Ansari.

Satyagraha acolyte endured would serve as a measure of his integrity and that of his cause… his target was the conscience of Britain.[158].

Two crucial points need to be considered here:

While the protesting Indians were asked to refrain from violence, armed protests, or any activity that resembled violence, the British were left free to use any violent method to suppress these protests, which is what they did. Whether it was Lathi[32] Charge, i.e., beating with sticks or horse riding police doing savage beating or even strafing unarmed men by aircraft as was done in '42. The Indians were cannon fodder in this method and always the victims.

The second key point that confuses about this policy is why the British were expected to have a conscience and be nice. They were in India as colonizers and had used all kinds of methods to achieve them. Wealth was generated, and the British were in India to create wealth, achieve a life of comfort and transfer the wealth to England. Morality had already been put on the back burner. *In no country in the world has a colonizer shown goodness of the heart.*

In 1919 firing by done on unarmed people at Jallianwala Baugh, which shook up India.

The Khilafat[33] the movement was started by Maulana Shaukat Ali and supported by Mahatma [34] Gandhi on November 24th, 1919, in a meeting of the Khilafat Conference. 'He proposed non-cooperation with the government to right the wrong done to the Ottoman Empire, which represented the Khilafat, the papacy of the Muslim world, and as a protest against the terrorist regime in Punjab.'[159] But when the

---

32. Wooden Stick

33. The flouting of the pledge made by Lloyd George, the British prime minister, not to dismember Turkey and not to take over the holy lands in the Hejaz had angered many Indian Muslims. (Bose, Opponent 48)

34. Great Soul -Title given by Tagore as stated in Keay, P 471

resolution was proposed, seven months had already passed from the Jallianwala massacre.

'The chosen issue of the Caliphate emphasized the allegiance of Muslims not to Indian sovereignty but to the external sovereignty of Dar-Ul-Islam, the world of Islam.'[160]

The movement had nothing to do with India. It was a protest against the termination of Ottoman Rule in Turkey, which had been defeated in World War I.

Due to support by Gandhiji, the movement was later projected as a freedom movement which it was not. It resulted in the Moplah Massacre of Hindus when the crowds were excited with fiery speeches.

'Khilafat movement wanted to invite the Amir of Afghanistan to invade India'![161] The British were vigilant, and this scheme of the Ali Brothers, which Gandhiji supported, did not succeed.

Calling India Dar-Ul-Harb, i.e., land controlled by Infidels, thousands migrated to Afghanistan.[162]

'As the non -cooperation movement wore on, the rallying cry of the Muslim leadership became Jihad against the British infidel…A fanatical Sufi of the Qadri tariqa Ali Muslaiyar preached Jihad with such venom and hatred that the population was made to believe that the rule of the Caliph would be soon established in Malabar and their struggle for Sharia law. Their fury rose against all infidels, resulting in large-scale rioting and massacre of Hindus in the Malabar'.[163]

Thus, a derivative of this Khilafat movement was the Moplah rebellion. '*The worst victims of their fanaticism were Hindus, who suffered rape, loot, conversion, and murder.*'[164] The Hindus had nothing to do with Khilafat, which was purely an Islamic movement.

Gandhi's support of these was his first significant encouragement to Muslims. But this appeasement soon became a regular feature of his policy.

*The Congress whitewashed the crimes against Hindus and said in its 1921 resolution number three..' The Moplah disturbance was not due to non-cooperation or the Khilafat movement..'*[165]

'Muslim league leader Maulana Hasrat Mohani said in a Muslim League meeting, 'Moplahs massacred Hindus because they were frightened. (Author's Question: Why were they frightened?) Because of an English detachment that suddenly appeared in the locality which somehow spread a rumor that the Hindu inhabitants had invited the English Army.'[166]

Jinnah, who had been a Congress leader so far, did not like the approach of Gandhiji of aligning with the Ali brothers and parted company with Congress.

The Khilafat movement ended when the Turkish people abolished Caliphate themselves, and Kamal Ataturk took power there.

The support of Congress changed the power equation of how the discussions were held among Hindus and Muslims. *'The succeeding forty years were to witness the congress and the British outbidding each other in concessions to communalism to win the Muslims to their side.'*[167]

Some other significant developments that took place in this period:

Subhas Bose returned to India at age 24 after qualifying as the 4th rank holder for I.C.S. He decided to devote his life to securing freedom for India and resigned from I.C.S.

When he returned to India, Bose went to see Gandhiji first. He asked him three questions, including how he expected complete independence in one-year, which Gandhiji had promised. He was not satisfied with the replies and later said,' *Either he did not want to give out all his secrets prematurely, or he did not have a clear conception of tactics whereby the hands of the Government could be forced.*[168]

Bose, after this, had gone and met Chittranjan Das and became his follower and assistant. Mr. Das had a massive following and was not committed to the creed of non-violence.

*Lloyd George, the British PM, had declared that 'The British Civil servants were the 'steel frame of the whole structure, and he did not care what you build on or of it: if you take that steel frame out, the fabric will collapse.'*[169]

To break the steel frame, Bose followed a similar strategy as the revolutionaries, but he made it broad-based with an all-India focus instead of an individual focus.

In aggressiveness and willingness to use violence to achieve his end, Bose can therefore be considered just one level different with the revolutionaries. His difference was that he worked with a strategy and later worked outside India; the British could not stop him, though, during the period of 1921-1930, he was arrested eleven times.

The second major event was the return of Vinayak Savarkar from the hell hole of Andaman Prison. The Savarkar brothers had been sent there after the British got Vinayak back from England and charged him with assisting in procuring a pistol. The Savarkar brothers, before this, had been involved in burning a bonfire of British clothes and encouraging the Swadeshi movement.

They had organized a group called 'Abhinav Bharat, 'held public meetings, protested the British occupation of India, and attended various conferences in Europe and Britain. In one such meeting, the flag of Independent India was unfurled by Madame Bhikaji Cama on August

18th, 1907. Madan Lal Dhingra, a student and part of Vinayak Savarkar's circle, decided to shoot Lord Curzon, who was back in England but ended up shooting the wrong person. Dhingra was hanged, and even Churchill was forced to say, 'Dhingra's last words are the finest ever made in the name of patriotism and even compared him with Plutarch's immortal heroes.'[170]

The British called him 'one of the most dangerous men that India has produced.'[171] Today he is known as Veer[35] Savarkar.

## *The Nationalist Stirrings intensify*

Under Montague -Chelmsford reforms religion-based electorate was accepted by Congress and Muslim League. When the Bill passed in the British parliament, which made laws for the India, quota was added for Europeans living in India and Christians in addition to what Congress and Muslim League had agreed in 1916.

These were formalized by the Government of India Act of 1919. This act also introduced the Dyarchy[36] System of governance, where the Central and state powers were bifurcated, and the civil service had defined rights that enabled them to control the elected representatives.

Also, the infamous Rowlett Act was brought into force, which gave draconian powers of arrest and detention to the Government.

Gandhiji launched a civil disobedience movement in 1921, promising freedom within one year. When the violence broke out in Chauri Chaura, where police had fired on unarmed protestors, the mob

---

[35.] Veer= Brave
[36.] Dyarchy: in which the more critical departments of Government would be reserved for the British governor and his civil servants. Indian ministers drawn from the elected members of the provincial legislative council could be put in charge of less sensitive departments. (Bose, Opponent, P48)

subsequently burnt the police station with the policeman inside who had taken shelter there; once their bullets were over, the disobedience movement was withdrawn.

Gandhiji was sentenced to six years in prison, though released early. He decided not to start any new movement till this period was over.

Meanwhile, Savarkar was released, put under severe mobility restrictions, and prohibited from undertaking any political activity. He spent the time building a Patit Pavan Mandir where the depressed classes – now called Dalit were the priests and organizing dinners where people from all communities ate together. Despite having qualified as a barrister, his degree was withheld. He was not allowed to practice and was neither allowed to publish any book.

Chittranjan Das, who was in Alipore jail, said about Gandhiji's method:' The *Mahatma opens a campaign in a brilliant fashion: he works it up with the unerring skill: he moves from success to success till he reaches the zenith of his campaign – but after that, he loses his nerve and begins to falter.*'[172]

Nehru was arrested in Nabha, a princely state where he had gone to investigate with some companions. He was marched through the streets of the town and thrown in jail, and in an oft-publicized incident, his father had to plead with the Viceroy to secure his release almost immediately.

Lala Lajpat Rai, the tallest leader of Punjab, was protesting against the Simon Commission, which had been sent to India to investigate the workings of Dyarchy, but the Commission had no Indian member. He was deliberately hit and died in about a fortnight from injuries sustained. He had been a vocal critic of separate electorates, which he had said it would never be abolished once established without a civil war if started.

'Gandhiji claimed Lajpat Rai's injuries were *good fortune.*' By demonstrating courage against force, the attack held out the prospect of a full transformation of authority and the conversion of Government by the sword into Government based on popular will and confidence. The assault, Gandhi said, 'part of the game we have to play.' Swaraj would only come when Indians were willing to die.'[173].

Aligarh School of Thought was formed at Aligarh Muslim University by Mohammed Ali Jauhar under Mohammed Habib.[37]. They set about whitewashing the Islamic atrocities against Hindus and sanitizing the records.[174]

In 1928 Motilal Nehru headed a committee that tried to create a framework for India within dominion status. Gandhiji stayed away from this. Motilal Nehru tried to unify Muslim League and Hindu Mahasabha on this but failed.

Bose and Gandhi's differences had started coming out in the open now. Bose was a General Secretary in 1929 along with Nehru.

The Viceroy in 1929 issued a statement about the possibility of dominion status, and Gandhiji decided to discuss this in the Lahore Session of Congress, while Bose wanted complete freedom. This was a significant difference between the two, Bose was dropped from the All-India Congress Committee, and Nehru was made Congress President.

This period in the late 1920s was also the most disturbed in Hindu-Muslim relations. After the Mopla Hindu massacre, in Kohat in N.W.F.P., about 20,000 Hindus were looted, pillaged, and plundered. Communal riots flared up in Delhi, Calcutta, Rawalpindi, etc.

---

[37] Father of S. Irfan Habib

As extra seats were allotted to Muslims more than a share of the population, the Hindus felt alienated and had been weakened.

In Dec 1926, Swami Shraddha Nand was murdered by a Muslim fanatic. Swamiji was involved in political activities and brought back into the Hindu fold some Muslims whose ancestors were forcibly converted to Islam by the Mughals. Gandhi widened the gulf between Congress and Hindu Mahasabha by calling the murderer 'dear brother' and rationalizing the murder.[175] Ambedkar expressed his critical feelings against Gandhiji.[176]

"On March 20th, 1927, a conference of Muslims met in Delhi to decide on the issue of separate electorates. The charter of demand now became broader: it included the separation of Sindh from Bombay; reforms for the Frontier and Baluchistan; representation by population in the Punjab and Bengal; and thirty-three percent reservations for the Muslims in the Central Legislature.[177]

In 1924 Dr. Keshav Baliram Hedgewar started Rashtriya Swamsevak Sangh -R.S.S. to foster nationalism.

In 1927 Dr. Munje, President of Hindu Mahasabha, played an important role in the formation of the Indian Military Academy in Dehradun to encourage increased recruitment of Indians in the officer corps of the Indian Army. This was to have a huge impact later as it was found that graduates of I.M.A., called Viceroy's commissioned officers, joined Indian National Army much more easily than officers commissioned at Sandhurst who were called Kings Commissioned officers.

In the 1929 meeting of Congress, a Purna Swaraj – full independence-day was declared. January 26th was to be henceforth celebrated as Independence Day. A pledge was endorsed to resist British rule and seek Purna Swaraj.

On April 6th, 1930, Gandhiji, by making a fistful of salt from the sea, violated the rules which demanded tax on salt. This is known as the 'Dandi March 'in history and had the participation of thousand and, when arrested, packed the prisons.

As usual, with all Gandhiji movements, the British successfully and easily suppressed this by violence. 'Congress committees were declared unlawful and special ordinances muzzled the press and restricted picketing.'[178].

Bose, who was Mayor of Calcutta, decided to Celebrate January 26th and was arrested. He spent twenty-four hours at Lal Bazar Police station and was beaten, and his two fingers of right hand sustained a fracture.

Bose and Lala Lajpat Rai remain the only prominent Congress leaders ever to be beaten.

Gandhiji was given a kid glove treatment by the British. When he was imprisoned, 'he had been given the same 'suite' of two roomy cells with wide front and roomy verandas and a small garden plot in front, which he had occupied in 1922. He was allowed all the exercise he wanted and had ample space for it and his bathroom facilities were scrupulously clean. A gaol steward did any shopping he needed, and six fellow convicts were detailed to perform duties for him, from the Indian who milked the goat to the two Europeans who each day carried his bed outside and back again.'[179]

Gandhi stuck a deal with the Viceroy Lord Irwin and, in exchange for prisoner release and other concessions, halted the civil disobedience. The settlement done by Gandhiji was so one-sided that even Nehru, who was his ardent supporter, had told him that he, Gandhi, had 'unwittingly sold India.'[180]

Lord Irwin is famous in history as foreign secretary Lord Halifax[38] who supported the appeasement of Hitler in 1938 with Prime Minister Chamberlain and for agreeing to Hitler's takeover of Czechoslovakia without even asking that country.

Bhagat Singh, who had protested in assembly with Batukeshwar Dutt, was punished by hanging. Gandhi's failure to intervene with Lord Irwin left significant discomfort in the country. Bose even organized a protest against Gandhiji when he came for the Karachi session of Congress, saying, "Gandhi, Go back."

Three round table conferences were held in London around this time. The first one did not invite Congress and was limited to the princes. Nothing was achieved. In the Second one, the sole representative was Gandhiji from the Congress side. At the same time, Jinnah, Master Tara Singh, and Ambedkar were other representatives. They were able to keep Gandhi's opinions down as all asked for more significant concessions for their communities. In the third, Congress refused to participate.

Therefore, nothing was accomplished by these, though they generated a lot of publicity and excitement. The tapes of Gandhiji dressed in a fakir's[39] garb still play to the audience.

'Gandhi was also a consummate showman and a shrewd politician with a knack for projecting himself in such a way as to attract the greatest possible attention in India and abroad. He gave press interviews in which he revealed a talent for self-dramatization, which made striking headlines. Even Gandhi's now familiar loin cloth was a prop in a well-thought-out piece of political stagecraft. Wearing it he appeared to the

---

[38] Sometimes it gets confusing as the same person ends up with multiple names when new titles are added in British set up.

[39] Usually meant saint who has given up on material aspects of life.

world as the living symbol of the semi-starved, almost naked villagers of India for whom he spoke, or so he said when he set out for Britain in July 1931, and then and later, he was taken at his word.'[181]

'However, much Gandhi had hoped for a more cooperation relationship with Delhi, the Government now had no use of his services as a Congress Spokesperson and negotiator. It was determined not to boost his reputation and strength by any pacts with him and it was now confident of its powers to crush civil disobedience at the outset and to let the constitution making process continue without Congress. Further Willingdon was no Irving. He felt that Gandhi was fundamentally two faced and while he may possibly have his saint like side, on the other he is the most Machiavellian bargaining little political humbug I have ever come across.'[182]

Unlike the sages of the earlier period whose projection was given by him and who lived an extremely simple life with bare minimum basic needs indifferent to worldly pleasures, his conditions were many and had to be met precisely. 'And of the elaborate simplicity of Gandhi's domestic arrangements, he may have observed sotto voce what Sarojini Naidu once remarked aloud: that it cost a great deal of money to keep the Mahatma in poverty.[183]

Bose had been exiled from India in 1933, and Mohammed Ali Jinnah was back in India.

A sick Bose who had been given a passport valid for only four countries and had no money as he was released only while the ship had sailed managed to get admitted in Vienna in the same sanitorium where Vitthal Bhai Patel, elder brother of Vallabh Bhai Patel was. His immigration was comfortable as Italian Consulate in Calcutta had informed his country. His stay was funded by his elder brother's friends and others.

Patel and Bose issued a strongly worded memo when Gandhiji withdrew from the movement in 1933.

Bose recovered after a while and started traveling in European countries when an official mistakenly issued him permission for other countries. Bose had several meetings with Mussolini, who was in power in Italy, and his son-in-law, Count Ciano, who was the second most powerful man at that time in Italy. He met Herman Goering, who became air chief later in Germany and was an influential leader in the Nazi hierarchy.

He traveled within Europe and tried to organize the India Leagues. He even helped Nehru with funeral arrangements when his wife passed away while in a Swiss Sanitorium.

Bose started writing 'The Indian Struggle' and met Emilie Schenkel, who later became his wife.[40] Bose also learned German.

In 1936, he was allowed to come back for a visit when his father was very sick. Unfortunately, he was too late, and his father left the world without meeting Subhas one last time. Bose was sent back into exile.

In 1938, he decided to return and was arrested upon return. Finally, the British released him, and he went back to Europe but returned when elected Congress President in his absence.

Meanwhile, there were other developments in India. Sir Mohammed Iqbal took up the idea of Pakistan, which was proposed by Chaudhary Rehmat Ali earlier. In the Allahabad session of the Muslim League in 1930, a formal demand was raised:

*'I would like to see the Punjab, Northwest Frontier Province, Sind, and Baluchistan amalgamated into a single State. Self-government within*

---

[40.] There are different views of different historians on this, in view of different statements of Bose also.

*the British Empire, or without the British Empire, the formation of a consolidated Northwest Indian Muslim State appears to me to be the final destiny of the Muslims, at least of Northwest India*[184].

*Says Historian Metcalf, 'After 1931, with a conservative-dominated national government in power (in England), they determined ways to devise ways of holding on to India, or as the Indian secretary, Samuel Hoare put it, of giving a semblance of responsible Government to Indians while 'keeping for ourselves the threads that really direct the system of Government.*[185]

*'This meant that Congress politicians should be diverted to and then kept bottled up in the provinces while the central Government, with power shared among Muslims, princes, and other groups such as Sikhs and untouchables, would be in the hands of those who could be relied upon to secure Britain's interests.*[186]

The British brought 'the communal award of 1932 ', allotting separate seats to Hindus, Sikhs, Europeans, and Muslims and adding a separate classification for Depressed Classes whom Gandhiji had named Harijan outside the Hindu seat quota.

Gandhiji went on a fast and had a settlement with Dr. Ambedkar called the Poona Pact -who had emerged as the leader of depressed Classes and was also nominated for the round table conference by the British. They settled to have a quota for Depressed classes within the Hindu category but were given a generous increase by reducing the quota for caste Hindus.

The British used this incident to project globally that India was a divided society.

The Congress party had to give comment on communal awards now.

The stand of Congress was decided on May 16th AICC meeting.' *A meeting of the AICC was held at Patna on May 16th to get the new program ratified. Gandhi attended it. The body set up a parliamentary board of twenty-five with Ansari. [41] as chairman to fight the coming elections, the working committee later declared its neutrality on the communal award, which led to the resignations of Malviya and his lieutenants, who wanted Congress to disown the award. But this was not possible because of Azad.[42] and other nationalist Muslims favored the award.'[187]*

Strangely, Mr. Ansari, a Muslim League president, chaired this committee. One of the most important voices in the committee was that of Maulana Azad, whose(negative) views were expressed clearly about Hindus in 1914. Patel has maintained that Azad only represented the Muslim viewpoint, and it was proved time and action by Azad's actions. *So Muslim League and Congress both represented Muslims here.*

Bose opposed communal award, and Pandit Madan Mohan Malviya resigned from Congress along with others when Congress declared its neutrality.

The communal award became a law when the India Act of 1935 was passed.

In his book 'Escape from Empire,' Professor Moore says, 'The 1935 Act gave the Muslims the best of both worlds. The minorities retained weightage, while in Bengal (where the European Community held 10% of the seats), the Muslims retained weightage, while in Punjab, a virtual statutory majority of 51.4% . The Muslim predominance in northwestern and eastern India was thus emphasized. At the same time,

---

[41.] Ansari is Mukhtar Ahmad Ansari, who was one of the founders of Jamia Milia Ismailia University in New Delhi and also had been president of All India Muslim League in 1920.

[42.] Azad is Maulana Abul Kalam Azad, who subsequently became the education minister of Free India and is widely credited with instituting in textbooks a Mughal-centric history with Crimes against Hindus and oppression whitewashed.

in the other provinces, they were given importance disproportionate to their numbers. As a result, there were inducements for Muslims to organize on communal lines for political ends.[188]

In 1937 elections were held for provincial assemblies. Gandhiji stayed away from the elections, but Nehru put his heart and soul into it, addressing meeting after meeting.

Dr. Ambedkar had formed the Independent Labor Party, which won 11 out of 15 seats in Bombay State. Later he was to focus only on the exclusive constituency of Dalits.

The Congress won six states on its own, and it was in the coalition in Assam and N.W.F.P.

In Punjab Unionist party formed the Government under Hayat Khan, and in Bengal, Fazlul Huq's Krishak Praja party.

Muslim League could win only 109 seats out of 482 reserved for Muslims rest going to the Unionist party and Krishak Praja, among others.

By 1937, Subhas Bose had recovered after his gall bladder removal surgery and was still in exile, in Europe; however, when he learned that he had been elected president of Congress in January 1938, leaving his book incomplete, he returned to India.

As president, he arranged a meeting of Congress's Chief ministers. He gave them an explicit thought to start planning for the future and create a path for reconstruction, industrialization, and a system that benefits have nots.

Bose and Gandhiji had considerable differences during this time. Bose was trying to discuss creating a United Front with Jinnah and Savarkar. When in 1939, the election for Congress President came about, Gandhiji put his candidate in opposition to Bose, and Bose won despite this. However, members of A.I.C.C., except for Subhas and Sarat, his brother, supported Gandhiji later and resigned. Rather than create further acrimony, Subhas Bose resigned.

In May 39, Bose formed a separate group within Congress -called Forward Block. For doing this, he was barred from holding any office in Congress for three years.

Jinnah joined forces with Mohammed Iqbal and demanded Pakistan, though he did not have power in any state at that time.

Leading Congress leaders had become Chief ministers and ministers and got involved in administration. Dyarchy had been removed in the 1935 Act, though the difference between central and state powers had been well defined.

# Chapter 8

# DO OR DIE

When 1939 started, the British were in a comfortable position in India.

The provincial governments were keeping the political parties busy, especially Congress, whose tall leaders were in Government now. Infighting between Bose and Gandhi was going on in early '39. Muslim League was trying to consolidate its position, and there was no movement against the British.

But War Clouds were gathering in Europe, and soon they would impact India as well.

When Lord Linlithgow, the Viceroy, included India in the war during September 39, he did not ask anyone in India.

Subsequently, Lord Linlithgow decided to have political discussions with various parties on war effort cooperation and started organizing India for war production. From the second week of October onwards, he discussed with Gandhi, Bose, Jinnah, Savarkar, Nehru, Ambedkar, and several others.

## War production:

The Corporate system at that time was that most companies were managed through managing agencies who collected a fee for managing a business. This enabled even owners of companies in England to have an India-based Managing Agency to look after business. Most Managing agencies were British, while there were some Indians like Tatas, Birlas, Goenkas, Bajaj, etc. Most of the Indian agencies were leading financiers of Gandhiji and Congress.

Massive orders were placed on them by the Government. The factories started humming with full activities and, in most cases, had to add an additional workforce.

The goods for war were bought by the Government of India and shipped to the British Government. For the British Government to avoid paying for these immediately, an innovative solution was created.

The Indian Government received credit for the goods supplied, which was used as an asset to issue new currency and increase the money supply. The money supply resulted in inflation in India, and as the war progressed, the rate kept going up. The wholesale price index was up 250% by the time the war ended.

When India became independent, a sum of £1.3 billion (approx. $ 5.2 billion) was due from England. It was later paid in small parts after deductions were done, adjusting liberal retirement benefits of British Nationals who had been serving in India, and so on. The Bombay Plan to use this money for Indian development, as made by Indian industrialists, fell by the wayside.

To Keep a lid on any activity that may distract from the war effort, the Defense of India Act was invoked, which gave broad powers of arrest, imprisonment, curtailment of freedom, etc.

As time went by during this period, India became more and more critical to the war effort. The recruitment and deployment of soldiers and officers from India was being done outside India. India was producing munitions and other materials. In World War II, India was to build aircraft, minesweepers, parachutes, garments, boots, etc., besides shipping sugar, tea, coffee, and such food products for the army.

When discussions started with the Viceroy, different political parties took different stands.

When the Viceroy met Gandhiji first, Gandhiji was inclined to offer support to the British as he had done in World War I. Still, when it was discussed among the Congress Working Committee, it was decided that Gandhiji should ask for an unequivocal declaration from the British about their intention to give freedom to India once the war ended.

When a discussion took place with Jinnah, he offered support without any qualifications. He pledged the loyalty of all Muslims everywhere and advised the British not to trust Congress.

Further, he asked: 'Muslim areas should be separated from 'Hindu India' and run by Muslims in collaboration with Great Britain.'[189]

Savarkar asked for: 'wanted a definite and immediate declaration of the grant of dominion status to India at the end of the war and to ensure the willingness of an Independent India in the future to continue a partnership in the commonwealth on equal terms.'[190]

Dr. Ambedkar: 'he disagreed with those who held that England's difficulty was India's opportunity and added that Indians should not go in for new masters. Concluding his statement, he stated that the duty of Britain towards India was to reassure her of the status she would occupy in the British Empire after the war was over and that India could not willingly and heartily fight for principles if she was not assured that the benefits of those principles would be extended to her when the war was won.[191].

The princes offered to support as they could, and their level of support differed.

The Viceroy decided to take support of the Muslim League and Dr. Ambedkar – who became a member of the Viceroy's council later- and princes. Congress was put on a back burner.

Bose proposed a motion for Congress to launch a civil disobedience movement, but the motion was defeated. Since Congress could not arrive at a conclusive decision with Lord Linlithgow, the Congress ministries resigned in protest.

At this time, the 'Congress ministries at this time exercised authority over three-fourths of the population of British India and ran eight out of eleven British provinces.'[192]

Says V. P. Menon, who was an advisor on constitution reforms to three viceroys and later as the key person reporting to Sardar Patel in the partition and integration of India in his book 'The Transfer of Power in India':

'Had it (Congress party) not resigned from its position of vantage in the provinces, the course of Indian history might have been very different.'[193]

'By resigning, the congress party showed lamentable political wisdom. There was little chance of its being put out of office: the British Government would surely have hesitated to incur the odium of dismissing ministries, which had the overwhelming support of the people. Nor could it have resisted a unanimous demand for a change at the center, a demand which would have been all the more irresistible after the entry of Japan into the war. In any case, it is clear that but for the resignation of the congress ministries, Jinnah and the Muslim league would have never attained the position they did.'[194]

Once the Congress ministers resigned, the power reverted to the Governor of each state, and the British were happy as this gave them complete freedom to act as they wanted.

Jinnah used this time to build up Muslim League in Punjab and Bengal and bring the other Muslim leaders to Muslim League Camp.

In 1940 he proclaimed in League Session at Lahore that 'the Muslims are a separate nation according to any definition of a nation and they must have their own homelands, their territory, and their states.'[195]

Citing here a part of the resolutions passed on March 26[th,] 1940, of the Muslim League:

'Resolved that it is the considered view of this session of the All India Muslim League that no constitutional plan would be workable in this country or acceptable to the Muslims unless it is designated on the following basic principle, viz. that geographically contiguous units are demarcated into regions which should be so constituted with such territorial readjustment as may be necessary that, the areas in which the Muslims are numerically in the majority as in the North Western and Eastern zones of India should be grouped to constitute 'Independent states' in which the constitutional Units shall be autonomous and sovereign.'[196]

'He suggested grouping the geographically contiguous areas in which the Muslims were in the majority as in northwest and eastern zones to constitute autonomous and sovereign states with such territorial adjustments as may be necessary."[197]

Muslim League national guards were created in Sept 1937 at the Muslim League convention. The stated objectives were developments of the community. Still, actual details were made clear by a subcommittee of the League in June 1939, which called for an organization and trained body of men for the protection of Muslim lives, property, and honor and for the defense of their rights against militant Hinduism in every part of India. This was to be the muscle power to ensure compliance with Jinnah's will in the future[198].

*'Jinnah was now escorted by volunteers of the Muslim National Guard in public meetings with drawn swords.'*[199]

Savarkar and Hindu Mahasabha, in a remarkable case of foresight, started a campaign asking Hindus to join the military. It is estimated that British Indian Army had at least 60-70% Muslims at this time. Jinnah was to claim later that this figure was 65%.[200] Eventually, Dr. Ambedkar was able to get the Mahar regiment started specifically for Depressed Classes, and there seems to be some result due to Savarkar that by 1943 the percentages had changed.

'The secretary of state for India stated in the House of Commons on July 8th, 1943, giving the composition as below: Muslims 34% , Hindus and Gurkhas 50%, Sikhs 10%, Christians and the rest 6%.

The result of this was when in 1947, the partition of assets was done between India and Pakistan, and army personnel were allowed to choose which country to go to; India was left with an army numerically bigger than Pakistan. 'The British staffed battalions were only six, while Indians in the Army were 373,570, out of whom 164,780 were Hindus, 135,268 Muslims and 35,390 Sikhs and 16,382 Christians, and others '.[201].

In December 1940, the British and United States entered a lend-lease agreement, which ensured Britain could get US supplies without immediately paying for them. India was added as one of the recipient countries from the US under the British ambit. The United States started sending men and materials to India.

In August 1941, Churchill and Roosevelt signed the Atlantic Charter, under which restoration of self-government was to be encouraged in the countries occupied by the Axis powers. But since India was already under British occupation, India was excluded from this purview as per British.

Netaji Subhas Chandra Bose had made a daring escape from India after he was released from prison after a hunger strike. He had started inspirational speeches from Germany aimed at the Indian public and was being widely heard in India. The general public widely appreciated his escape from India and the use of German help, and it also put pressure on Gandhiji to do something.

When Japan threatened to invade India, President Roosevelt increased the pressure to give dominion status to India. President felt that this would allow some expectations of Indians to be met and ensure that they supported the allied cause against Japan.

President Roosevelt also sent his representative, Colonel Johnson, to check the progress.

Churchill was against giving independence to India and opposed Roosevelt when he had proposed, but he could not stop the United States nominee from going to India. The proposal envisaged setting up a constitution-making body at the war's end and creating a new Indian Union as a dominion, among other details.[202]

Sir Stanford Cripps came to India and discussed broadly with various Indian political leaders.

Cripps's mission was a typical British attempt to show carrots and use sticks. It offered an increased say in the Government. Still, it asked the congress party to accept the right of each state or princely state to choose if they wanted to stay independent by joining India or Pakistan, which would have effectively Balkanized India. Cripps's focus was getting a constituent assembly which would have led to more discussions, acrimony, and a few more years being passed in limbo. Repeatedly he said, 'I am convinced that India's salvation remains in a constituent assembly. '[203]

Cripps Mission failed. Moore says, 'American and Indian opinion guessed at the truth that Cripps was undermined by colleagues who did not want to bring the Raj to an early end.[204] Even before the final collapse, 'highly placed Americans were angrily saying that Churchill had butted in to prevent a reasonable settlement.'[205]

With the failure of Cripps Mission, Gandhiji said,' it was as clear as crystal that the British Government did not propose to give up the power, they possess over the four hundred million unless the latter develop strength enough to wrest it from them.'[206]

Commenting on the mission, Nehru had said, 'there was no certainty that Britain would withdraw from India after the war in view of their repeated broken promises as regards to India's future self-government and accused England of 'deliberately driving a wedge between Hindus and the Muslims.[207]

Bose, speaking on Azad Hind Radio from Germany on March 31, 1942, commented upon Cripps's mission, exposing the British policies. He said:

'British politicians and the British propaganda machine have been continually reminding us since 1939 that the Axis Powers are a menace to India, and now, we are being told that India is in danger of an attack by the enemy. But is not this sheer hypocrisy?

India has no enemies outside her own frontiers. Her one enemy is British imperialism, and the only adversary that India has to get rid of is the perpetual aggression of British imperialism. It was the British Government that declared India to be a belligerent power, against the will of the Indian people, and has since then been forcibly exploiting the resources of India for Britain's war purposes[208].'

## Call for Do and Die:

Meanwhile, Gandhiji had continued discussions with the Viceroy. Since Viceroy had already received Muslim and Princes' support, he did not feel the need to accept any of Gandhiji's proposals which kept getting rejected on some ground or the other.

Gandhiji also gave some opinions and views which disturbed the British. At a time when they were trying to fight with Germany with every single asset and skill at their disposal, Gandhiji advised the British to give up the fight against Hitler and Mussolini: *'Let them take possession of your beautiful island... allow yourself, man, woman, and child to be slaughtered, but you will refuse to owe allegiance to them.'*[209]

*'He advised the Jews in Germany to offer passive resistance to the Nazi regime – and to give up their lives as sacrifices.'*[210]

'Gandhiji was worried that in their frustration, some congressmen might go too far and start an agitation against the Government, which he had promised the Viceroy he would discourage. So, he worked out a strategy that would enable the Congress party to show to the public that it was giving no quarter to the British authorities and yet take no action that would really hinder the war effort, a stand Subhas Chandra Bose compared to 'running with the hare and hunting with the hound.'[211]

Gandhiji now decided on a new tack. He wrote to the Viceroy that he did not want to embarrass the British Government, but this desire could not be carried to the extent of 'Congress party committing Hara-Kiri.'[212]

Thus 'Individual peaceful disobedience was launched on October 17th, 1940. At peak, 15000 people were arrested. The movement dragged on for a year with dwindling numbers participating. The effect on India's war effort was nil.'[213]

However, When Gandhiji met the Viceroy on November 4[th,] he promised to Viceroy to continue to work toward a settlement.

'The official history of the Civil Disobedience Movement 1940-41 argues that Gandhi was basically motivated by a desire for attention; Gandhi was content with his primary object of keeping Congress before the public eye'. Gandhi's perverse childishness was further revealed by his insistence on overcoming all opposition from his colleagues and establishing himself as the dictator of Congress policy. How such a determination to hoard all the glory for himself could be reconciled with the admission that he was a trusted leader with a peculiar influence over the public mind who was able to lead a movement when the hearts of the people were not in it -could be explained only by the ease with which many people in this country can be persuaded not to think for themselves '.[214]

Gandhi had been vacillating on the issue of Pakistan.' In the Harijan of May 4th, 1940, he had said, 'I would any day prefer Muslim rule to British rule... the partition proposal had altered the face of the Hindu Muslim problem... Pakistan cannot be worse than foreign domination. His earlier statements were vague at best where he had said, 'As a man of non-violence, I cannot forcibly resist the proposed partition if the Muslims of India really insist upon it.. but I can never be a willing party to the vivisection.' On another occasion, he had declared in a rather emotional manner, 'Vivisect me before you vivisect India. But in the wake of no negotiations with the League or the Government on the matter or even a public admonishment of the Pakistan Scheme, the Congress, and Gandhi were giving mixed signals on their acquiescence.'[215]

Congress was fast losing its relevance. When the All-India Congress Committee convened in Allahabad on April 29th, 1942, only about 100 of its 370 members attended that first session, reflecting the apathy of most members and the alienation of many from their leadership.[216]

Why did Gandhiji launch the August '42 movement?

An analysis reveals five reasons:

1. Congress was fast becoming irrelevant. Its membership was showing a downward trend. From a high of 4.5 million in 1938-39 its membership in 1941-42 was reduced to just 1.5 million.

2. The British considered Gandhiji irrelevant and were firmly in control with the support of the Muslim League, princes, and imposition of Defense of India Act. He had to establish his relevance again.

3. Jinnah and the Muslim League were catching all the attention.

4. Gandhiji, who was perpetually kept in the news by something or the other despite launching only two major protests so far, was getting ignored in the press.

5. Subhas Bose had escaped to Germany and started his broadcasts and caught the imagination of the public. There was a possibility that Subhas Bose might end up on the borders of India and start liberating India with his armed forces.

Says Wofford, who later became a U.S. Senator, in the book India Afire:

'The fact that Indian public opinion ran with Subhas probably played a major role in deciding Gandhi to launch his Quit India campaign when. Gandhi feared that if Britain did not declare immediate independence and permit Congress to organize resistance, the Indian masses would give overwhelming support to Bose and welcome Japanese armies as liberators.'

Thus, Gandhiji, who had missed the opportunity to strike against the British in 1940 when they were at their weakest and most vulnerable, now had to start a movement to keep himself relevant.

On August 8[th,] 1942, he spoke to the All-India Congress Committee: Selected Excerpts[217]:

*'A non-violent soldier of freedom will covet nothing for himself; he fights only for the freedom of his country. The Congress is unconcerned as to who will rule when freedom is attained. The power, when it comes, will belong to the people of India, and it will be for them to decide to whom it is placed in the entrusted...*

*Our quarrel is not with the British people; we fight their imperialism. The proposal for the withdrawal of British power did not come out of anger. It came to enable India to play its due part at the present critical juncture. It is not a happy position for a big country like India to be merely helping with money and material obtained willy-nilly from her while the United Nations are conducting the war. We cannot evoke the true spirit of sacrifice and velour so long as we are not free.*

*As a matter of fact, I feel myself to be a greater friend of the British now than ever before. One reason is that they are today in distress. My very friendship, therefore, demands that I should try to save them from their mistakes.*

*To those who have been indulging in a campaign of abuse and vilification, I would say, "Islam enjoins you not to revile even an enemy. The Prophet treated even enemies with kindness and tried to win them over with his fairness and generosity. Are you follower of that Islam or of any other? If you are followers of true Islam, does it behave you to distrust the words of one who makes a public declaration of his faith?*

*To the Quaid-Azam[43], I would say: Whatever is true and valid in the claim for Pakistan is already in your hands. What is wrong and untenable is in nobody's gift so that it can be made over to you.*

*I would say: "I consider myself a friend of Musselman's. Why should I then not give expression to the things nearest to my heart, even at the cost of displeasing them? How can I conceal my innermost thoughts from them? I should congratulate the Quaid-i-Azam on his frankness in giving expression to his thoughts and feelings, even if they sound bitter to his hearers.*

*Rajaji said: "I do not believe in Pakistan. But Musselman's ask for it, Mr. Jinnah asks for it, and it has become an obsession with them. Why not then say, "yes" to them just now? The same Mr. Jinnah will, later on, realize the disadvantages of Pakistan and will forgo the demand." I said: "It is not fair to accept as true a thing which I hold to be untrue and ask others to do say in the belief that the demand will not be pressed when the time comes for settling in finally. If I hold the demand to be just, I should concede it this very day.*

*It is for that reason that I say to Jinnah Saheb, "You may take it from me that whatever in your demand for Pakistan accords with considerations of justice and equity is lying in your pocket; whatever in the demand is contrary to justice and equity you can take only by the sword and in no other manner."*

*I, therefore, want freedom immediately, this very night, before dawn, if it can be had. Freedom cannot now wait for the realization of communal unity. If that unity is not achieved, sacrifices necessary for it will have to be much greater than would have otherwise sufficed. But the Congress must win freedom or be wiped out in the effort.*

---

[43]. A title given to Mr. Jinnah in the Urdu press and subsequently popularized by Gandhiji.

*Here is a mantra, a short one, that I give you. You may imprint it on your hearts and let every breath of yours give expression to it. The mantra is: 'Do or Die.' We shall either free India or die in the attempt; we shall not live to see the perpetuation of our slavery. Every true Congressman or woman will join the struggle with an inflexible determination not to remain alive to see the country in bondage and slavery.*

*Soldiers, too, are covered by the present program. I do not ask them just now to resign from their posts and to leave the army. The soldiers come to me, Jawaharlal, and the Maulana say: "We are wholly with you. We are tired of the Governmental tyranny." To these soldiers, I would say: You may say to the Government, "Our hearts are with the Congress. We are not going to leave our posts. We will serve you as long as we receive your salaries. We will obey your just orders but will refuse to fire on our own people."*

*There are representatives of the foreign press assembled here today. Through them, I wish to say to the world that the United Powers, who somehow or other say that they have a need for India, have the opportunity now to declare India free and prove their bona fides.*

*I have been the author of the non-embarrassment policy of Congress, and yet today, you find me talking this strong language. I say it is consistent with our honor. If a man holds me by the neck and wants to drown me, may I not struggle to free myself directly? There is no inconsistency in our position today.*

*Do or Die.*

*I have pledged the Congress, and the Congress will do or die.*

*The full speech can be read at* https://archive.pib.gov.in/quitindia75/ vignettes/QIMSpeech.pdf.

'In the early hours of the following morning, all members of the working committee and most other Congress leaders, both national and provincial, were arrested, and the All-India Congress Committee and the provincial Congress committees were declared unlawful associations. This swift stern action was taken with the unanimous approval of all the eleven Indian members of the Executive Council.[218]

Gandhiji was put in Aga Khan's palace which had nine large bedrooms in Poona. The British i.e. Government of India paid Rs. 12000 per year as rent for this property which had seventy acres of grounds and twelve gardeners to tend them... His wife Kasturba and four other close persons and disciples were sent to live with them.[219] Seventy-eight police personnel and a jailor supervised this.

Nine senior leaders, including Azad and Nehru, were put in Ahmednagar Jail in comfortable surrounding with conveniences. They ate food served on China plates, cooked by a designated cook, played games, and read newspapers, and held discussions among themselves.

Says Durgadas: 'The Quit India movement then degenerated into an ill-organized mass upheaval lit up as much by acts of surprising individual ingenuity and heroism as by crude outbursts of incendiarism and looting. Anti-social elements and the communists indulged in violence and destruction.'[220]

'The Government estimated that rebels had fully or partially destroyed 208 police stations, 749 government buildings, 332 railway stations, and 945 post and telegraph offices. They had also derailed 66 trains, Sabotaged railway lines in 411 places, and severed 12000 telephone lines.'[221].

'Brutal forces were used to suppress. It is estimated that 'between 1000-2500 protestors were killed and 60,000 to 90,000 imprisoned, with the conditions in goal for most volunteers appalling. *An American observer compared the state of prisons to concentration camps.*[222]

The protesting people were strafed by aircraft, and many died, whose details were not revealed.[223] 'The Congress Party was outlawed throughout British India.'[224]

Subhash Bose spoke to Indians on August 17th 1942 on radio. Speaking from Germany on August 31st, 1942, Subhas Bose asked all segments of Indian to join the struggle: *'I appeal to the Jamiat-ul-Ulema, the old representative organization of the Ulemas or the Muslim divines of India, led by that distinguished patriot and leader Mufti Khifayat Ullah. I appeal to the Azad Muslim League, another important organization of the nationalist Muslims of India. I appeal to the Akali Dal, the leading nationalist Sikh party of India. And last but not least, I appeal to the Praja Party of Bengal, which commands the confidence of that province and is led by well-known patriots. I have no doubt that if all these organizations join in this struggle, the day of India's liberation will be drawn nearer*[225]*.*'

Bose asked, 'In this guerrilla war the tactics of dispersal have to be employed'[226].

He further asked Indians to stop cooperating with the British and suggested an Economic boycott.

By Mid -September, the big demonstrations were suppressed, and Gandhi, Nehru, and other leaders had resumed their well-rehearsed jail regimes of reading, Writing, and exercise.'[227]

Durgadas, the renowned journalist, confirms: 'Thus, by September 1942, the Quit India movement was broken, and the British had imposed a sullen, frustrated quiet in India by using all instruments of suppression.[228].

The use of the Sword once again saved the Raj, just like in 1857.

Dr. Ambedkar had not joined the movement. He said 'The Quit India campaign turned out to be a complete failure. It was a mad venture and took the most diabolical form. It was a scorched earth campaign in which the victims of lootings, arson, and murder were Indians, and the perpetrators were congressmen.'[229]

Muslim League and Hindu Mahasabha did not join the movement either.

Says Penderel Moon, who was in Indian Civil service: 'The movement, though in certain limited areas intense and dangerous, aroused in the country as a whole less widespread national feeling than the civil disobedience movement of 1930 and was brought to an end very much more quickly.'[230]

Says Historian Tunzelmann, 'Effectively, Congress had given the Raj an excuse to imprison hundreds of its leaders, including Gandhi and Nehru – who, according to his sister, was almost thankful for it, *so uncomfortable had he felt opposing the war effort.* The resolution could never have succeeded; Britain could not evacuate India in the middle of the Second World War, with Japan looming on its eastern front. But the space created in politics by the congress leaders being in prison gave the Muslim League its chance to rush in.'[231]

Even Gandhian K M Munshi said this: *"The "Quit India" movement launched by the Congress in August 1942 under Mahatma Gandhi's leadership proved disastrous to India's immemorial integrity. It cemented the alliance between the bureaucrats and the communalists.'*[232]

Revolutionaries took up the movement, and Jaiprakash Narain, who was loved and esteemed by Gandhi, repudiated the Gandhian non-violence and spoke the language of violence, and adopted a revolutionary program.[233] Later, he organized a network of secret organizations to carry out his program of People's Revolution.

Says historian Majumdar 'Gandhi had fired his last shot (of course figuratively) in 1932 and missed. For ten years, he remained a non-combatant. On August 8[th,] 1942, he again pulled his trigger, but there was no shot because he forgot to put any cartridge in the chamber. Then he retired, finally from direct and active participation in India's struggle for freedom…. Both Gandhi and Congress offered apologies and explanations for the madness that seized the people participating in it. The resolution of the working committee of the congress dated 11th December 1945 referred to the events during 1942-1945 'as a series of impulsive and heroic, albeit undirected aberrations. Jayaprakash Narain most emphatically asserts that 'to **fasten the August program on Gandhiji is a piece of perjury of which only the British ruling class can be capable.**'[234]

In October 1943, Under Secretary of State for war in the Churchill cabinet, Page Croft wrote to Churchill. The failure of Gandhi to rouse India against the King-Emperor is one of the happiest events of the war.'[235]

In September'42, as a concession to Indians, Sir Ramaswamy Mudaliyar and Maharaj Jam Saheb of Navanagar, who were invited to join the war cabinet in London, reached there. Churchill said when he had met them in the background of disturbances(the Quit India movement) in India.' if we ever have to quit India, *We shall quit it in a blaze of glory, and the chapter that shall be ended then will be the most glorious chapter of that country's not merely in relation to the past but equally in relation to the future, however distant that may be.*'[236]

This was a prophetic statement. Though Churchill was able to subdue Gandhiji but he did not expect that it will be Bose's efforts that will force the British hand but the British were able to retain the illusion of control till the last day.

# EPILOGUE

An uneasy calm had been forced on India by the end of 1942. The Do or Die movement, better known later as Quit India, was Congress's last movement before Independence. Gandhiji remained comfortably ensconced in Aga Khan's Palace till mid '44, when he was released due to ill health (He had Malaria). In 1943, he undertook a fast of 21 days as well. It kept the newspapers busy, and everybody was concerned for his health, but it achieved nothing. Ordering his release, Lord Wavell, the Viceroy, 'secured *a letter offering withdrawal of civil disobedience and full cooperation in the war effort should a declaration of Indian Independence be forthcoming.*'[237]

Nehru and other leaders were released after the war was over on the Western Front in Mid '45.

They were called to Shimla in the summer of '45 to discuss reconstituting the Viceroy's advisory council, the body that governed India. There is no evidence of any British plan to give freedom to India soon.

The Japanese invasion of India via Burma did not happen in '42 because the monsoon had started, and in those few months, it became impossible to use the land route.

In 1943, fighting the United States, the Japanese suffered multiple setbacks in the war in the Pacific, including the significant battle of Midway, which led them to divert naval resources away from India and Asia.

By the time the war ended, because of the way purchases were financed by issuing more currency, India had runaway inflation. In 1943, there was a massive famine in Bengal due to rice imports having stopped from Burma, available rice bought for the army, and Churchill's refusal to send from other sources.

In 1943, Subhas Bose reached Singapore from Germany, accompanied by Abid Hassan, his aide. Meanwhile, the Japanese had put resources in I.N.A.,and everything received a boost with Bose being there.

Bose in Singapore formed Arzi Hukumat e Azad Hind - the Provisional Government of Free India, in October 1943. Indian National Army, made largely of ex-British Army soldiers, was its armed wing. Nine countries recognized this, and Japan handed over the Andaman and Nicobar Islands to this government. It had a bank, its own currency, postage, etc., while fighting a war and offices in entire Southeast Asia. Indians in these areas liberally supported this with money and manpower.

Subhas Chandra Bose was the Prime Minister and Supreme Commander of I.N.A. and was treated as head of State by Japan and other countries who had recognized this Government.

Singapore and Malaya remained with the Japanese till their surrender in August 1945. The atomic bombs were dropped on Hiroshima and Nagasaki, which largely vaporized these cities and it led the Japanese Government to surrender.

At that time, Netaji Subhas Bose's Indian National Army was fighting alongside the Japanese to liberate India via Burma. They had reached Moirang in Assam and had not only planted an Indian flag there, but I.N.A. had also liberated substantial Indian territory under it as well. For almost three months, the I.N.A. and the Japanese battled Allied powers, but with American aircraft in India and the Japanese air force severely debilitated, the Allies flew sortie after sortie and bombed out the I.N.A. and the Japanese. The battle in this sector was won by the Allies due to U.S. resources and Air Force.

Most of the I.N.A. soldiers who were on the frontlines were destroyed and disintegrated. The British brought the remaining Ex-British Army soldiers back to India; some are believed to have been shot with a court martial on the spot. More than half of the I.N.A. were former British Indian Army personnel -the rest were Indians from Malaya, Singapore, Thailand, etc. The others who were not ex-British Indian Army were left to go to their respective countries and families.

Brought back to India, the British initially decided to put eight officers on trial- the first three were a Hindu, a Sikh, and a Muslim. Thus, Col. G.S. Dhillon, Maj Gen. Shahnawaz Khan, and Col. P.K. Sahgal were tried in a military court. For the first time since 1858, they made the mistake of trying people of Hindu, Sikh, and Muslim religion simultaneously. Further, the British had lost the aura of invincibility. Netaji had inspired I.N.A. soldiers so much that even in defeat, they remained staunchly committed nationalists. The British interviewing them had started classifying them as white, grey, and black, depending on their nationalist feelings. There were vast numbers of grey and black.

By the time the trial ended in end December 1945– an ailing Bhulabhai Desai representing the first three I.N.A. veterans had destroyed the case of the prosecution and established that I.N.A. was a legitimate army of a legitimate country that had received recognition from nine countries and cited examples from the United States and French history, among others. He spoke extempore for ten hours over two days. Unfortunately, this patriot who brought out the story of I.N.A. in front of the world left the world before he could see an independent India. The three soldiers were cashiered and given life imprisonment, but recognizing the mood of the country, the British army chief waived the imprisonment and retained only the financial part of the decision.

The trial being at the Red Fort in Delhi was widely covered.

When the results of the provincial elections came in 1946, riding a wave of popularity, having embraced I.N.A. as its own, talking about it in public meetings, and frequently ending the meetings with Jai Hind-the I.N.A. greeting, Congress had swept the elections. Hindu Mahasabha, whose leader Savarkar was seriously ailing with two heart attacks in quick succession, and Dr. Ambedkar's party were swept aside. Muslim League secured the majority in Bengal but could only become the single largest party in Punjab and Sind, losing N.W.F.P. to Congress.

The Navy rebelled in February '46, the Air Force rebelled in the next few days, and rebellion started in a few army units.

Police and post office served strike notices, and port workers went on strike. Besides, industrial units in virtually all sectors either served notices or went on strike.

The whole country started agitations. I.N.A. had psychologically dealt the fatal blow to British Rule by destroying the British aura of invincibility. The ability of the British to impose violence was seriously suspect due to the army's loyalty in doubt. The British records confirm this.

This is how the seeds of Independence that were put in the ground by the Indian National Army came to fruition. It did not matter that

Subhas Bose was not there. The hands of the British were still forced. In just Seven months after the trial of I.N.A. veterans began, the quickly unfolding events led to the British decision to withdraw and communicate the same to Indians to quieten the agitated country.

India had become impossible to manage. The British decided to show that they are leaving amicably and handed over power to the Congress party and Muslim League as soon as it could be done.

Congress, Muslim League, and others were invited to form an all-party Government in the Centre. Nehru took an oath[44] on September 2nd, 1946, as Vice President[45] (Prime Minister). Muslim league had not joined as they could not settle on power share, but after the butchery of Direct Action Day, Congress met all the demands, and they joined the government, which governed India till August 15, 1947, when India and Pakistan became two countries based on religion.

Says historian Wilson 'Prime Minister Clement Atlee and the Secretary of State Lord Patrick -Lawrence knew the British had no choice but to retreat. But they believed retreat could occur while maintaining the illusion of a consciously planned transfer of sovereign power; they wanted to propagate the myth, *in other words, that the Empire ruled until the last, that it had willingly transferred the power of its own volition.*'[238]

Confirms historian Hutchins '*in reality, the British withdrawal was the result of pressure exerted from within India... The British left India because Indians had made it impossible for them to stay.*'[239]

This illusion of peaceful transfer enabled the British to work out how to delay and minimize the payment of almost £1.3 Billion (approx. $5.2 billion) owed to India for supplies during World War II, besides

---

44. Oath of office taken in the name of British King.
45. Lord Wavell, the Viceroy, was the President.

protecting British commercial interest and the wealth and pensions of British employees in India. The British Indian Army, which was still all over the Middle East and Southeast Asia, was replaced by conscription in Britain– a first in peacetime. The amount of $5.2 Billion was huge at that time. This should be seen in the light that a loan of $5 billion from the U.S. and Canada led to the reconstruction of Britain after World War II and was paid back in installments till 2005.Many favors were done to the British. The British MI-5 was allowed to operate in India till 1960 as per an agreement with Nehru and entry of Hindu sages to Nagaland was banned as per British Christian group demand- which led to religious conversions on a massive scale in Northeast India. The British companies retained their Indian companies as before.

India became a dominion on August 15, 1947, and after the constitution was adopted on January 26th, 1950, it became a sovereign republic. January 26[th,] twenty years earlier, this was the date when Purna *swaraj*-full independence demand was made.

The nationalists in India adopted 'Jai Hind'[46] as the standard greeting of armed forces and law enforcement and the flag of free India flies on Red Fort just as Subhas Bose visualized. On August 8th, 2022, Prime Minister Narendra Modi inaugurated his statue at the heart of New Delhi's power center, from where the Supreme Commander of the Indian National Army, the first Prime Minister of undivided India, and the person most responsible for India's freedom, now stands guard.

---

46. Jai Hind= Victory to Hindustan or Glory to India.

# SOURCES

**Books:**

Ahmed, Ishtiaq: Pakistan the Garrison State, @2013, Oxford University Press

Ambedkar. B.R.: Pakistan or the partition of India @1945 Kalpaz Publications Delhi

Ayer S.A.: Unto him a witness, Thacker& Co. Ltd. Bombay

Balakrishnan Sandeep: Seventy Years of Secularism

Bandyopadhyay, Sekhar: From Plassey to Partition and After, @2015, Orient Black Swan

Barrow, Ian: The East India Company 1600-1858, Indianapolis @2017

Bayly Christopher and Harper Tim: Forgotten Armies the fall of the British Asia 1941-1945 @Belknap Press of Harvard University Press, Cambridge MA

Bose Subhas Chandra:CrossroadsCollected works @1960 Netaji Research Bureau, Calcutta

Bose, Subhas Chandra: The Indian Struggle 1920-1942, @1964 Asia Publishing House

Brendon, Piers: The decline and fall of the British Empire 1781-1997 @2007, Alfred A Knopf New York

Brown, Judith: Gandhi-prisoner of Hope @1989, Yale University Press

Craig, William: The fall of Japan, @1997 Galahad Books New York

Dharampal: Despoliation, and defaming of India, Goa @1999

Dixit Sanjay: Unbreaking India, @2020 Garuda Prakashan, New Delhi

Durgadas:India from Curzon to Nehru and after, @1969 Rupa, New Delhi

Edwardes: Michael, Last years of British India, @1963 Cassell &Co. Ltd. London

Elkins, Caroline:Legacy of Violence, @2022 Alfred A Knopf, New York

Elst,Konrad:Gandhi to Godse, @2001, Voice of India

Fay, Peter Ward:The Forgotten Army, India's Armed Struggle for Independence 1942-1945 @1995 The University of Michigan Press, Ann Arbor MI USA

Gordon: Leonard A, Brothers against the Raj, @2015 Rupa, New Delhi.

Ghosh K.K.: The Indian National Army @1969, Meenakshi Prakashan, Meerut

Gilbert, Martin: The First World War @1994 Henry Holt and Co. New York

Gilbert, Martin: The Second World War @1989 Henry Holt and Co. New York

Hutchins, Francis G: India's Revolution -Gandhi and the Quit India Movement, @1973, Harvard University Press

Howitt William:The English In India, London @1839

James, Lawrence: Raj the making and unmaking of British India @1997 St Lawrence Press, New York

James, Lawrence: The Rise, and Fall of the British Empire, @1996 St Martin's Press, New York

Keay, John: India a history @2000 Grove Press, New York

Keer, Dhananjay:Ambedkar, his life and mission @1954 Popular Prakashan

Kumar, Dr. Susmit: Re-evaluating Gandhi, @2023, Garuda Prakashan, New Delhi.

Kirby, Major General Woodburn:The War Against Japan, India's most dangerous hour Volume II, @1958 Her Majesty's Stationery Office, London

Kulkarni, V.B:Pilgrims to Freedom – K.M. Munshi @1959 Publications Division

Kuhlmann, Jan: Netaji in Europe, @2012, Rainlight/Rupa New Delhi

MacMunn G.F. Major: the Armies of India @1911, Adam and Charles Black, London

MacMunn, George: Lt. General, The Martial Races of India, Sampson Low, Marston & Co. Ltd. London

Majumdar, R.C:History of the Freedom Movement in India @1975, Firma K.L.M. Pvt. Ltd, Calcutta

Menon V.P.: The transfer of Power in India @2020 Sani H Panihwar

Metcalfe Barbara and Metcalfe Thomas: A concise history of India @2002 Cambridge University Press

Mills, James: The History of British India Vol I-VI, London @1826

Moon, Sir Penderel: The British Conquest and Dominion of India, @1989, Duckworth, London

Moore, R.J.:The Escape from Empire @1983 Clarendon Press, Oxford. U.K.

Oak, Nilesh: Did the Mahabharata war happen? The mystery of Arundhati.

Pandit Sunderlal: @2018How India lost her freedom, Mumbai,

Phillips, The East India Company: @1940 Manchester University Press

Prasad, Bisheswar: Expansion of the Armed Forces and Defense organization @1956 Combined Inter-Services Historical Section, India and Pakistan.

Planning Commission: Subhas Chandra Bose- Pioneer of Indian Planning @1997 New Delhi.

Piers, Brendon: The decline and fall of the British Empire @2007 Alfred Knopf

Publications Division: Selected Speeches of Subhas Bose @1962 New Delhi.

Raghavan, Reed, Sir Stanley: The Indian Year Book 1919, Times of India, Bombay

Risley H.H. And Gait, E.A.:Census of India 1901 @1903 Office of the Superintendent of Government Printing Calcutta.

Sampath, Vikram: Savarkar, Echoes from a forgotten past @2019 Penguin Viking

Sampath, Vikram: Savarkar, A contested Legacy, @2021, Penguin Random House

Sarila, Narinder Singh: The Shadow of the Great Game @2005 Carrol & Graf, New York

Sarkar, Sumit: Towards Freedom Part I @Oxford University Press

Singh, Jaswant:Jinnah-India-Partition-Independence @2009 Rupa

Sitaramayya, B. Pattabhi:The History of the Indian National Congress (1885-1935) @1935 Published by the Working Committee of the Congress

Taylor, A J P: English History 1914-1945@1965, Oxford University Press, New York

Toye, Richard: Churchill's Empire @2010, St. Martin's Griffin, New York

Tunzelmann, Alex Von: Indian Summer @2007 Henry Holt, and Co. New York

Wilson, Jon,:The Chaos of Empire, @2016 Public Affairs, New York

Warren, Alan:Burma 1942 The Road from Rangoon to Mandalay @2001, Continuum International Publishing, London-New York

Wolpert, Stanley:Shameful flight, the last years of the British Empire in India, @2006 Oxford University Press

# DOCUMENTS FROM OTHER SOURCES

## British

https://www.open.ac.uk/researchprojects/makingbritain/content/
round-table-conferences-1930-1932

https://api.parliament.uk/historic-hansard/commons/1946/feb/22/
royal-indian-navy-mutiny

## Others

https://history.state.gov/milestones/1937-45/atlantic-conf

https://ccnmtl.columbia.edu/projects/mmt/ambedkar/web/readings/
Simhadri.pdf

(Criminal Tribes Act of 1871)

http://www.columbia.edu/itc/mealac/pritchett/00litlinks/txt_azad_
congress_1940.html

https://pakistanspace.tripod.com/archives/40lahore.htm

http://www.columbia.edu/itc/mealac/pritchett/00islamlinks/txt_
iqbal_1930.html

## Indian

www.Anindianinside.wordpress.com

www.dharmadispatch.in

www.dharampal.in

https://archive.pib.gov.in/quitindia75/vignettes/QIMSpeech.pdf

https://www.constitutionofindia.net/historical_constitutions/
the_congress_league_scheme_1916__inc___aiml__1st%20
January%201916

www.knowingmahadev.wordpress.com

https://www.onlinejewelryart.com/2020/10/gold-price-chart-100-
years.html

## Exchange rate conversions from:

https://www.uwyo.edu/numimage/currency.htm

# NOTES AND REFERENCES

[1]    As cited in Tunzelmann,Indian,P 48

[2]    Prasad, Expansion, PP 9,10

[3]    As Cited in Prasad, Expansion PP 12,13

[4]    Kirby, Japan, P 47

[5]    Bayly and Harper, Forgotten, P 33

[6]    Bayly and Harper, Forgotten, P 33

[7]    As cited in Brendon, Decline and Fall P 423

[8]    Brendon, Decline and Fall PP 422,423

[9]    As cited in Brendon, Decline and Fall P 424

[10]   Bayly and Harper, Forgotten, P 107

[11]   Craig, Fall, 306

[12]   As cited in Bayly and Harper, Forgotten P 114

[13]   Summarized from Bayly and Harper, Forgotten PP 115-116

[14]   Bayly and Harper, Forgotten P 116

[15]   Gilbert, Second, P 276

[16]   Gilbert, Second, P276

[17]   Bayly and Harper, Forgotten P 117

[18]   Bayly and Harper, Forgotten, P 117

[19]   As cited in Bayly and Harper, Forgotten, P 119

[20]   Gilbert, Second, PP 282-283

[21]   Gilbert, Second, P282

[22] Bayly and Harper, Forgotten, P 129

[23] Bayly and Harper, forgotten, P 129

[24] Craig, Fall, P 307

[25] Brendon, Decline and Fall, P 428

[26] Bayly and Harper, Forgotten, P 143

[27] Bayly and Harper, Forgotten, P 147

[28] As cited in Brendon, Decline and Fall, P 429

[29] As Cited in Gilbert, Second, P 300

[30] Kirby, Japan, P XVI

[31] Warren, Burma, P 32

[32] Warren, Burma, PP34-35

[33] Warren, Burma, P 35

[34] Kirby, Japan, P 8

[35] Kirby, Japan, P 26

[36] Kirby, Japan, P 93

[37] Summarized from Kirby, Japan PP 92-96

[38] Warren, Burma, P 163

[39] Warren, Burma, P 167

[40] Gilbert, Second 314,315

[41] Gilbert, Second, P315

[42] Gilbert, Second, P 321

[43] Warren, Burma, P 155

[44] Elkins, Violence P 358

[45] Wilson, Chaos, P 449

[46] Elkins, Violence P 282

[47] Bayley and Harper, Forgotten, P 187

[48] Warren, Burma, P 230

[49] Warren, Burma, P 250

[50] Warren, Burma, P 184

[51]   Warren, Burma P 183

[52]   Warren, Burma, P 183

[53]   Warren, Burma, P 183

[54]   Summarized from Warren, Burma PP 189-190

[55]   Summarized from Warren, Burma PP 189-190

[56]   Summarized from Warren, Burma P 192

[57]   Summarized from Warren, Burma PP 194-199

[58]   Warren, Burma, P 200

[59]   Warren, Burma, P 200

[60]   Warren, Burma, P 237

[61]   Wilson, Chaos, P 448

[62]   Ward Fay, Forgotten P 99

[63]   Kirby, Japan, P 126

[64]   As cited in Hutchins, India's, P 194

[65]   Bayly and Harper, Forgotten, P 192

[66]   Wilson, Chaos, P 448

[67]   Wolpert, Shameful, P 39

[68]   As cited in Hutchins, India's, P 193

[69]   Wilson, Chaos, PP448,449

[70]   As cited in Bayly and Harper, Forgotten P 191

[71]   Gilbert, Second P 303

[72]   As cited in Kirby, Japan, P 131

[73]   Gilbert, World War I, PP 130-131

[74]   Ibid P 131

[75]   Gordon, Brothers, P 130

[76]   Ayer, Unto, P xxii

[77]   Ayer, Unto P 214

[78]   Elkins, Violence, P 397

[79]   Bose, Crossroads P 33

[80] Planning, Planning PP28-29

[81] Bose in a letter to his elder brother Sarat Bose written while in England, Pilgrim 234

[82] Bose, Pilgrim, in a letter to his elder brother Sarat Bose written while in England P 234

[83] Ghosh, Indian 141

[84] Wilson, Chaos, P 401

[85] Gordon, Brothers, P 147

[86] Toye, Subhas 119

[87] Toye, Subhas, 118

[88] Summarized from Kuhlmann, Netaji, P 39

[89] Summarized from Kuhlmann, Netaji,PP 39-40

[90] Gordon, Brothers P 296

[91] Gordon, Brothers P 297

[92] As cited in Kuhlmann, Netaji, P 101

[93] Publication Division, Speeches, P 146

[94] Gilbert, World War II, P 278

[95] Bayly and Harper Forgotten P 147

[96] Bayly and Harper, Forgotten P 147

[97] Bayly and Harper, Forgotten P 256

[98] Gordon, Brothers 285

[99] As cited in Sampath, Savarkar, P 330

[100] Ibid P 330

[101] Sunder Lal, India P16

[102] Sunderlal,India P 16

[103] James, Raj P9

[104] Moon,Dominon and Conquest P12

[105] Barrow, East India43

[106] Keay India P 388

[107] Moon, Dominion and Conquest P 51

[108] Brendon, Decline and fall 34

[109] Keay, Honorable, P 304

[110] Sunder Lal, India P181

[111] Sunder Lal, India P 188

[112] James, Raj P34

[113] Orne, Indostan Vol II PP 187-89 cited by Sunder Lal, India P 199

[114] Howitt, English P 47

[115] Sunderlal, India P 204

[116] Sunderlal India P 255

[117] Barrow, East India, 49

[118] James, Raj, P 42

[119] Brendon, Decline and fall P 34

[120] Sunderlal on P 264 citing from Torrens, Empire in Asia PP 82-83

[121] Dharampal,Despoilation,P58

[122] Barrow, East India 88, Brendon, Decline and fall P 47

[123] Moon, Dominion and conquest 291

[124] Moon, Dominion and Conquest P 289

[125] Brendon, Decline and FallP47

[126] Sunderlal, India P 484

[127] James, Raj, P 47

[128] Philips, The evolution P 505

[129] Philips, The Evolution P 505

[130] Macmunn, Martial Races, P 172

[131] MacMunn, The Martial Races, P 224

[132] Summarized from Rishley and Gait, Census of 1903 PP 542-544

[133] Moon, Divide, P 11

[134] Summarized from Wilson, Chaos, P 368

[135] Dixit, Unbreaking P 45

[136] Sitaramayya, Congress, P 10

[137] Ibid P 11

[138] Ibid P 11

[139] Summarized from Elkins, Violence, P 216

[140] Wilson, Chaos P 337

[141] Bandyopadhyay, Plassey, PP 230-231

[142] Reed, Stanley, Indian Year Book 1919, PP 564,565

[143] https://www.onlinejewelryart.com/2020/10/gold-price-chart-100-years.html

[144] Summarized from Rishley and Gait, Census, 1903

[145] Elkins, Violence PP 77-78

[146] Summarized from Durga Das, Curzon to Nehru P 33

[147] Summarized from Ambedkar, Pakistan, PP 428, 434

[148] Edwardes, Last Years, P 41

[149] James, Rise and Fall P 367

[150] Taylor, English, P 85

[151] Durgadas, Curzon P 45. The book uses the term terrorists for the revolutionaries.

[152] Elkins, Violence, P 130

[153] Durgadas, Curzon, P 46

[154] Gilbert, World War I, P 131

[155] Bose, Struggle, P 48

[156] Bandyopadhyay, Plassey, PP 308,309

[157] Bose, Struggle, P 45

[158] James, Rise and Fall P 416

[159] Durgadas Curzon to Nehru P 52

[160] Keay, India, P 479

[161] As cited in Ambedkar, Partition, P 83

[162] Elst, Gandhi, P 76

[163] Dixit, Unbreaking P 28

[164] Durgadas Curzon P 81

[165] Dixit, Unbreaking, P 24

[166] Dixit, Unbreaking, P 29

[167] Durga Das, Curzon to Nehru P 43

[168] Bose, struggle, P 43

[169] Durgadas, Curzon, P 45

[170] Sampath, Savarakar, P 171

[171] Sampath, Savarkar, P 198

[172] Gordon, Brothers, P 61

[173] Wilson, Chaos, P 428

[174] More details in Balakrishnan, Sandeep, 70 years of secularism

[175] Sampath, Savarkar contested 88-100

[176] Sampath, Savarkar contested 91

[177] Singh, Jinnah, P 359

[178] Keay, India P 487

[179] Brown, Gandhi, P 244

[180] Toye, Churchill P 177

[181] James, Raj, P 524

[182] Brown, Gandhi, P 262

[183] Ward Fay, Forgotten P 192

[184] http://www.columbia.edu/itc/mealac/pritchett/00islamlinks/txt_iqbal_1930.html.

[185] Metcalf and Metcalf, Concise History, P 191

[186] Metcalf and Metcalf, Concise History, P 191

[187] Durgadas, Curzon P 162

[188] Moore, Escape P 5

[189] Sarila, Shadow P 42

[190] Sampath, Savarkar Contested, P 251

[191] Keer, Ambedkar, P 326

[192] Sarila, Shadow P 35

[193] Sarila, Shadow P 36

[194] Sarila, Shadow PP 37-38

[195] Sarila, Shadow, P 51

[196] https://pakistanspace.tripod.com/archives/40lahore.htm

[197] Sarila, Shadow P 51

[198] Sarkar, Towards, P 181

[199] Summarized from Sarila, Shadow, P 60

[200] As cited in Wolpert, shameful, P 47

[201] Ahmed, Pakistan P 60

[202] Summarized from Durgadas, Curzon P 205

[203] Pattarambiah, Congress Book 2, P 187

[204] Moore, Escape P 12

[205] Toye, Churchill's P 224

[206] Menon, Transfer P 145

[207] Sarila, Shadow P 131

[208] Ayer, Selected Speeches 137

[209] Tunzelmann, Indian P 93

[210] Tunzelmann, Indian P 94

[211] Sarila, Shadow P 58

[212] Sarila, Shadow P 58

[213] Sarila, Shadow PP 58-59

[214] As cited in Hutchins, India's P 171

[215] Sampath, Savarkar Contested, P 334

[216] Wolpert, Shameful, P 39

[217] The full speech can be accessed at https://archive.pib.gov.in/quitindia75/vignettes/QIMSpeech.pdf.

[218] Moon, dominion, P 1115

[219] Kumar, Re-evaluating, P 304

[220] Durgadas, Curzon, P 211

[221] Raghavan, India's, P 272

[222] Wilson, Chaos, P 450

[223] Summarized from James, Raj, P 566

[224] Durgadas, Curzon, P 210

[225] Ayer, Selected Speeches 150

[226] Ayer, Selected Speeches 151

[227] Bayly and Harper, Forgotten, P 249

[228] Durgadas, Curzon, P 211

[229] Ambedkar, Partition P 407

[230] Moon, Conquest P 1117

[231] Tunzelmann, Indian P 107

[232] Munshi, Freedom P 101

[233] Majumdar, Freedom Movement Vol III, 667

[234] Majumdar, Freedom Movement, Vol III, P 673

[235] As cited in Kumar, Re-evaluating Gandhi, P 309

[236] Toye, Churchill's P 227

[237] Durgadas Curzon P 213

[238] Wilson, Chaos, P 471

[239] Hutchins, India's, P 1